Out of Poverty

This book provides a comprehensive defense of Third World sweatshops. It explains how these sweatshops provide the best available opportunity to workers, and how they play an important role in the process of development that eventually leads to better wages and working conditions. Using economic theory, the author argues that much of what the anti-sweatshop movement has agitated for would actually harm the very workers they intend to help by creating less-desirable alternatives and undermining the process of development. Nowhere does this book put profits or economic efficiency above people. Improving the welfare of poorer citizens of Third World countries is the goal, and the book explores which methods best achieve that goal. *Out of Poverty* will help readers understand how activists and policy makers can help Third World workers.

Benjamin Powell is the Director of the Free Market Institute at Texas Tech University and a Visiting Professor in the Rawls College of Business. He is a past president of the Association of Private Enterprise Education and a Senior Fellow with the Independent Institute. Professor Powell is editor of *Making Poor Nations Rich: Entrepreneurship and the Process of Development* (2008) and coeditor of *Housing America: Building Out of a Crisis* (2009). He is the author of more than fifty scholarly articles and policy studies. His primary fields of research are economic development, Austrian economics, and public choice. Dr. Powell's scholarly research on sweatshops has been published in *Comparative Economic Studies*, the *Journal of Labor Research*, *Human Rights Quarterly*, and the *Journal of Business Ethics*. His research findings have been reported in more than 100 popular press outlets, including the *Wall Street Journal* and the *New York Times*. He received his PhD in economics from George Mason University.

Cambridge Studies in Economics, Choice, and Society

Founding Editors

Timur Kuran, Duke University
Peter J. Boettke, George Mason University

This interdisciplinary series promotes original theoretical and empirical research as well as integrative syntheses involving links between individual choice, institutions, and social outcomes. Contributions are welcome from across the social sciences, particularly in the areas where economic analysis is joined with other disciplines, such as comparative political economy, new institutional economics, and behavioral economics.

Books in the Series:

Terry L. Anderson and Gary D. Libecap, *Environmental Markets: A Property Rights Approach* 2014
Morris B. Hoffman, *The Punisher's Brain: The Evolution of Judge and Jury* 2014
Peter T. Leeson, *Anarchy Unbound: Why Self-Governance Works Better Than You Think* 2014
Benjamin Powell, *Out of Poverty: Sweatshops in the Global Economy* 2014

Out of Poverty

Sweatshops in the Global Economy

BENJAMIN POWELL

Texas Tech University

CAMBRIDGE
UNIVERSITY PRESS

32 Avenue of the Americas, New York NY 10013-2473, USA

Cambridge University Press is part of the University of Cambridge.

It furthers the University's mission by disseminating knowledge in the pursuit of education, learning and research at the highest international levels of excellence.

www.cambridge.org
Information on this title: www.cambridge.org/9781107688933

First published 2014

A catalogue record for this publication is available from the British Library

Library of Congress Cataloguing in Publication data
Powell, Benjamin, 1978–
Out of poverty : sweatshops in the global economy / Benjamin Powell,
The Free Market Institute, Texas Tech University.
  pages   cm. – (Cambridge studies in economics, choice, and society)
Includes bibliographical references and index.
ISBN 978-1-107-02990-3 (alk. paper)
1. Sweatshops.   2. Anti-sweatshop movement – History.   3. Economic
development – Moral and ethical aspects.   I. Title.
HD2337.P694   2014
331.25′6–dc23   2013043747

ISBN 978-1-107-02990-3 Hardback
ISBN 978-1-107-68893-3 Paperback

Contents

Figures

Tables

Acknowledgments

My first debt for this book is owed to David Skarbek. Now a lecturer at King's College London, he was an undergraduate student in an international economics class I taught at San Jose State University in 2004. He approached me with a desire to write a term paper that we might jointly turn into a scholarly journal article. I suggested working on an empirical investigation of sweatshop wages. We eventually published the paper that evolved out of that project in the *Journal of Labor Research*. It was my first sweatshop-related research.

That initial research led to many invitations to give public lectures about sweatshops. I have given lectures to, or participated in debates in front of, civic groups, professional associations, and, mostly, college and university student groups. I resist the urge to try to name each audience I have lectured to about sweatshops because I will surely leave some out. It now numbers at least scores and probably somewhere in the hundreds. This book is a direct result of the public lectures and the feedback I received at them. In the course of my lectures I found myself addressing more and more aspects of sweatshops that went beyond topics I had been able to address in scholarly journal articles. Ultimately, I decided that it was time to write a book on the topic that could more fully elaborate the points I was making in my lectures. I am indebted to the students and faculty members who helped to arrange these many lectures and the participants, both hostile (and there were many of them) and sympathetic, who provided feedback over the last decade.

Although most of this book is new work, it does draw on my prior research. I'm indebted to coauthors Matt Zwolinski, J. R. Clark, and David Skarbek for their contributions to that research. Chapter 7, in particular, draws heavily on work that Matt did with me, and many of the ideas appearing in that chapter were initially his. I also thank Giancarlo Ibarguen and his staff at the Universidad Francisco Marroqui'n for the help they provided J. R. Clark and me in surveying workers and visiting factories in Guatemala. Some of that research appears in Chapter 5. I'm also grateful that the editors of the *Journal of Business Ethics*, *Comparative Economic Studies*, the *Journal of Labor Research*, and *Human Rights Quarterly* all saw fit to publish my research on sweatshops.

I'm grateful to the Earhart Foundation for financial support that allowed me to write much of this book over the course of two summers. I thank Nicolas Cachanosky, Rick Weber, Tylor Orme, Rosolino Candela, and Audrey Redford, who provided valuable research and manuscript preparation assistance over the course of this project while they were working as my graduate assistants at Suffolk University. And I thank Linley Hall who provided valuable editorial assistance.

I'm grateful that Cambridge University Press senior editor Scott Parris and series editors Timur Kuran and Peter J. Boettke believed in this project from the beginning and encouraged me to pursue it. I also thank Kristen Purdy, who replaced Scott, and her staff for seeing the project through to completion, and I thank David Theroux and Roy Carlisle who were able to involve the Independent Institute in the publication of this book. I also thank two of the three anonymous Cambridge University Press reviewers for valuable feedback on the first half of the manuscript. I'm indebted to Jeffery Rogers Hummel for providing valuable feedback on the historical chapter in this book and to Matt Zwolinski and Mark LeBar for helping me avoid saying anything (hopefully) that philosophers would consider stupid in the chapter on ethics. The greatest thanks go to David Skarbek and Josh McCabe, who read the entire manuscript and provided valuable feedback that often substantially altered my presentation of the material.

Over the last decade I have benefited from discussions with some great colleagues at San Jose State University, Suffolk University, and now Texas Tech University. I have also benefited from teaching with excellent faculty members at summer seminars for the Independent Institute, Foundation for Economic Education, the Institute for Humane Studies, and the Fund for American Studies. Susan Love Brown, with whom I lectured at a summer seminar, gave me the idea for the title of Chapter 4, but most of these colleagues influenced my thinking on these issues in more subtle ways, which were nevertheless important.

I also thank my graduate students who have gone on to become professors, or are in the process of doing so: Nicholas Cachanosky, Rosolino Candela, Joe Connors, Nick Curott, Tom Duncan, G. P. Manish, Ryan Murphy, Malavika Nair, Colin O'Reilly, Audrey Redford, Matt Ryan, Nick Snow, Evgeny Vorotnikov, and Rick Weber. Working with them has pushed me to grow as a scholar.

I'm very fortunate to have gone to graduate school at George Mason University at a time when there was a great cohort of PhD students who would all go on to become accomplished academics. Thank you Ed Stringham, Scott Beaulier, Peter Leeson, Chris Coyne, Anne Bradley, Virgil Storr, and Ryan Oprea for always challenging me to become a better economist. The greatest thanks is reserved for Peter Boettke. Over the past fourteen years he has been the best mentor any young economist could ask for. I would not be where I am today if it was not for his guidance and encouragement.

Finally, I thank my wife Lisa for her love, patience, and continued support, and for putting up with endless conversations about economics.

Preface

Christian Hansen oiled the machinery and fixed the belts at the Waterhead Mills in Lowell, Massachusetts, for a dozen years. The mill processed corduroy, velvet, and finished cotton goods. It ran on steam power until 5 PM, after which some of the machines changed over to electric power. Part of Christian's job was to change over the motors at 5 PM. On March 16, 1920, Christian went about his usual work routine. Shortly after 5 PM, he threw one of the switches to turn on the electric power. The nearby compensator box had not been properly grounded and was leaking electricity. Christian was hit with 550 volts of electricity and died on the spot.

At about the same time, Leona Gagne began working at the Cardinal Shoe Factory in nearby Lawrence, Massachusetts. She worked up to ten hours a day, sometimes six days per week. The pay was modest, but as her son Paul recalls it, "It wasn't bad for what she did. And the money helped put my brother and me through school."

I knew Leona as "Nana." She was my great-grandmother. Christian was my stepfather's great-grandfather. However, in the pages that follow, I defend the type of "sweatshop" jobs in which Leona and Christian worked. I argue that the jobs are the best realistic alternative available to the workers employed in them and that such jobs are part of the very process of economic development that allows the descendants of Leona, Christian, and their counterparts toiling in Third World sweatshops today to enjoy a higher standard of living with safer, better-paying jobs.

As an economist, I am hardly alone in making this defense, and I am not the only such economist who had ancestors work in sweatshops. Another economist described the situation his immigrant mother, Sara Friedman, was in when she arrived in the United States around the turn of the last century:

Very shortly after my mother's arrival, she started earning her own living by working as a seamstress in a "sweatshop." In view of the bad reputation of sweatshops, it is interesting that I never heard my mother make a negative remark about her experience. On the contrary, she regarded it as enabling her to earn a living while she learned English and became adjusted to the new country.[1]

Her son, Milton, would go on to teach at the University of Chicago and win a Nobel Prize in economics. When economists, such as Milton or I, defend the existence of so-called sweatshop jobs, it is not because of any lack of caring or compassion for the workers. Rather, our defense stems from an understanding of the laws of economics. The laws of economics do not put profits over people. They dictate which policies will help poor workers and which policies will harm them. If you want to help today's Leonas and Christians in the Third World, you should be interested in learning how economic theory relates to sweatshops. I sincerely hope this book helps you in that endeavor.

---

[1] Milton and Rose Friedman, *Two Lucky People* (Chicago: University of Chicago Press, 1998), 20.

1

Introduction

Abigail Martinez earned only 55 cents per hour stitching clothing in an El Salvadoran garment factory. She worked as long as eighteen hours a day in an unventilated room; the company provided undrinkable water. If she upset her bosses they would deny her bathroom breaks or demand that she do cleaning work outside under the hot sun. Abigail's job sounds horrible. However, many economists defend the existence of sweatshop jobs such as hers.[1]

"In Praise of Cheap Labor: Bad Jobs at Bad Wages Are Better Than No Jobs at All." Only a right-wing free-market apologist for global capitalism could ever write an article with such an appalling title, right? Wrong. Those are the words of a darling of the left, *New York Times* columnist and Nobel Prize winning economist Paul Krugman.[2] Krugman argues that critics have not found a viable alternative to these Third World sweatshops and that the sweatshops are superior to the rural poverty the citizens of these countries would otherwise endure.

Krugman is not alone. After Haiti's devastating earthquake, Paul Collier, author of *The Bottom Billion*, prepared a report for the United Nations outlining a reconstruction plan for the country.[3] The development of a Haitian garment industry was central in his plan. He argued that Haiti had good access to key markets and that "due to its poverty

---

[1] Facts in this paragraph are reported by Leslie Kaufman and David Gonzalez in a *New York Times* article on April 24, 2001, entitled "Labor Standards Clash with Global Reality."

[2] Paul Krugman, "In Praise of Cheap Labor: Bad Jobs at Bad Wages Are Better Than No Jobs at All," *Slate Magazine*, March 1997.

[3] "Haiti: From Natural Catastrophe to Economic Security," *A Report for the Secretary-General of the United Nations*, January 2009. Retrieved from http://www.focal.ca/pdf/haiticollier.pdf.

and relatively unregulated labour market, Haiti has labour costs that are fully competitive with China." Collier essentially outlined a sweat-shop model of economic development for Haiti.

Wages and working conditions in Third World sweatshops are appal-ling compared to the wages and conditions that I and most readers of this book are likely used to. Any decent human being who has witnessed poor workers toiling in a sweatshop should hope for some-thing better for those workers. So why have people such as Krugman, Collier, and many other economists from across the ideological spec-trum defended sweatshop employment? These economists have defended sweatshops because they are the best achievable alternative available to the workers who choose to work in them, and the spread of sweatshop employment is part of the process of development that can eventually lead to higher wages and improved working conditions.

How bad are the alternatives to sweatshops? In Cambodia, hundreds of people scavenge for plastic bags, metal cans, and bits of food in trash dumps. Nicholas Kristof reported in the *New York Times* that "Nhep Chanda averages 75 cents a day for her efforts. For her, the idea of being exploited in a garment factory – working only six days a week, inside, instead of seven days in the broiling sun, for up to $2 a day – is a dream."[4] Other common alternatives are subsistence agriculture, other informal sector work, begging, or even prostitution.

Recent international trade did not invent poverty. The history of humanity is one of poverty. In most places in the world, for most of human history, people had low incomes, worked long hours, and had short life expectancies. Poverty has been the norm and unfortunately still is the norm for much of the world's population. Although First World citizens often express a desire for an end to poverty, normal Third World rural poverty does not raise the sense of moral outrage that sweatshops do.[5] People become more outraged about sweatshops

---

[4] Nicholas Kristof, "Inviting All Democrats," *New York Times*, January 14, 2004.
[5] I continue to use "Third World" to describe the poorer countries of the world even though it is a bit dated and out of fashion. "Developing world" is often inaccurate, as many countries are actually getting poorer, and besides, rich countries are still devel-oping, too. I do not like "less developed" because then their problem is insolvable – some countries will always be relatively less developed no matter how rich they get. Underdeveloped is true of all countries, even rich ones, compared to their potential. I will continue to use Third World until someone comes up with something more satisfactory.

because the poor workers are toiling for our benefit. Unfortunately, that moral outrage can lead wealthy consumers and their governments to take actions that, although they may assuage their feelings of guilt, make Third World workers worse off by taking away their ability to work in a sweatshop and throwing them into an even worse alternative such as scavenging in a trash dump.

This book provides a comprehensive defense of sweatshops. I do not deny that sweatshops have wages far below the levels in the developed world. Nor do I deny that sweatshops often have long and unpredictable working hours, a high risk of injuries on the job, and generally unhealthy working conditions. Sweatshops also sometimes deny lunch or bathroom breaks, verbally abuse workers, require overtime, and break local labor laws. Despite these atrocious conditions, sweatshops are still in the best interest of the workers who choose to work in them.

Sweatshops that coerce their workers with the threat of violence or use the local government to do it for them are the one type of sweatshop I condemn and will not defend. That is slave labor and has no place in a moral society. That type of sweatshop cannot be defended by the economic arguments made in the remainder of this book. If a worker must be coerced with the threat of violence to accept a job, then that job is obviously not the best alternative available to that worker – otherwise they would have voluntarily taken the job.

Despite all of their drawbacks to Western eyes, most sweatshops with low wages and poor working conditions are places where workers voluntarily choose to work. Rarely do employers actually use the threat of violence to obtain employees. Admittedly, workers' other options are often much worse. A starving person with no alternative employment is likely to take a very bad job if offered one. But that does not change the fact that the bad job was his best option. To help sweatshop workers, more options are needed. Unfortunately, much of the anti-sweatshop movement is aimed at taking away the sweatshop option without replacing it with something better that is actually attainable.

Economic theory is used throughout this book, but nowhere do I advocate "economic efficiency" as my ethical standard. The welfare of poor workers and potential workers in the Third World is the standard used throughout this book. Nowhere do I favor economic efficiency, the welfare of Western consumers, or profits at the expense of workers. The welfare of the worker is the end; the crucial question is the means to achieve it. Any serious anti-sweatshop activist *must* be concerned with this question. Market forces motivate how firms interact with workers; thus, activists need to appreciate the role they play as a means to helping workers. Economics puts limits on peoples' utopias. Wishing does not make things so. Economic theory forces us to examine how actions taken by activists, nongovernmental organizations (NGOs), governments, consumers, and others will impact the incentives of businesses that employ sweatshop workers. Unfortunately, many actions for which the anti-sweatshop movement has agitated adversely impact incentives and harm worker welfare.

Chapter 2 introduces the anti-sweatshop movement. It is a diverse movement that includes celebrities, ministers, students, politicians, intellectuals, unions, and consumer activists who advocate for policies such as international labor standards and minimum or "living" wages in the name of helping workers. When a country fails to adopt their favored policies, they will sometimes advocate imposing trade restrictions against the country. In other cases, they may simply protest an individual firm or company that uses sweatshop labor, which can lead to consumer boycotts.

But what effect will such actions have on the welfare of workers? To answer this question we need to understand the economic forces that determine sweatshop wages. Chapter 3 explains how the maximum wage that workers can earn is limited by their productivity and their next best alternative employment limits the minimum wage they will voluntarily accept. Unfortunately, many actions taken by activists do nothing to raise these two bounds; in fact, they often advocate policies that would push wages above the maximum level employers are willing to pay. As a result, sweatshop wages do not improve; instead, the jobs disappear. The second half of Chapter 3 examines possible exceptions scholars have raised to the basic theory outlined in the first half of the chapter.

If sweatshop workers lose their jobs, what are their other alternatives? Are they all destined to scavenge in trash dumps? Chapter 4 systematically investigates how sweatshop wages compare to alternative employment in the countries where they operate. It compares the apparel industry wages in sweatshop countries, and those in the very firms that the Western press has identified as sweatshops, with the average income in each country. The apparel industry, and even the firms recognized as sweatshops, usually pays more than the average national income. Sometimes they pay two, three, or even four times the average pay in the country. Sweatshop jobs are not just better when compared to scavenging in trash dumps. They are better than many of jobs in the countries where they are located.

Even some critics of sweatshops will admit that the wages paid by sweatshops are better than worker alternatives. But then they claim that the real problem is the deplorable health and safety standards in these factories. But health and safety standards and working conditions more generally, are intimately tied to wages. Employers care about the total cost of compensating workers but care little about how that cost is divided between wages and other forms of compensation. Workers do care. As a result, firms have every incentive to make the mix of compensation match the preferences of their employees. As Chapter 5 argues, health and safety standards are low because the workers' overall level of compensation is low, and they prefer the vast majority of that compensation in wages. The best cure for low health and safety standards is the process of economic development.

What about the children? In 1993 U.S. Senator Tom Harkin proposed banning imports from countries that employed children in sweatshops. In response, Bangladeshi firms laid off 50,000 children. What was their next best alternative? According to the British charity Oxfam, many of them became prostitutes or starved.[6] Prostitution and starvation are clearly worse alternatives than sweatshop labor. Chapter 6 explains how all of the preceding arguments apply to children as well as adults and how economic growth leads to the abolition of child labor.

What about ethics? Don't workers have a "right" to better treatment or higher wages? Even if the sweatshop is the workers' best alternative, is it not still unethical to buy their products? Chapter 7 makes an ethical case for buying sweatshop products on consequentialist grounds, considering issues of background injustice and exploitation.

Anti-sweatshop activists often seem to forget that they live in countries that once had widespread use of sweatshops, too. Chapter 8 will provide some historical perspective by examining the role that sweatshops played in the development of the United States and other wealthy countries. Sweatshops are important in creating new technology and

---

[6] See Paul Krugman, "Reckonings; Hearts and Heads," *New York Times*, April 22, 2001.

capital that eventually raises labor productivity. This process of economic growth leads to improved wages and working conditions. Although the process took more than 100 years in the United States, it can happen much more rapidly today because the world has a greater amount of capital and technology that it can export to these poor countries. Witness the rapid rise of the Asian tigers and China's growth today. Chapter 8 will also demonstrate that the level of development the United States had achieved before adopting more stringent labor standards was much greater than the level of development in sweatshop countries today. If the United States had adopted more stringent standards when it was as poor as the sweatshop countries today, it would never have grown to be as rich as it is now.

Chapters 9 and 10 describe how sweatshops can be replaced with better alternatives. Chapter 9 builds on the previous chapter by describing how the process of economic development takes place and the necessary enabling environment that allows a country to grow out of sweatshops.

Sweatshops may be the best option currently available for workers, but any moral person would aspire to help improve those conditions. What good can activists possibly do? Chapter 10 outlines positive steps activists can take to improve the lives of sweatshop workers. "Ethical" branding is one option, and there is a role for profit or nonprofit firms in monitoring this labeling. Trade policy and immigration law are other areas in which activism could help. All the actions outlined in this chapter would help improve the lives of poor sweatshop workers, but they will be marginal compared to the main cure.

The very process of industrialization and development, of which sweatshops are part, is ultimately the cure for sweatshops. As capital accumulates, technology improves, and as workers build skills productivity rises. As firms compete with each other for the productive workers, total compensation gets bid up. This process raises wages and improves working conditions, and it occurred in virtually all of the wealthy countries in the world today.

I have studied sweatshops for the past ten years. In that time I have become convinced that many well-meaning people advocate actions that are detrimental to the lives of sweatshop workers because they do not understand the economic forces that govern the creation of sweatshops and their alternatives. The remainder of this book explains these economic forces and illustrates them with the best available evidence. This book is intended for a wide audience that includes economists, other social scientists, and policy makers. It is also intended for the general public, particularly people who have been active in the anti-sweatshop movement and genuinely care about the welfare of impoverished sweatshop workers.

Rather than hold protests that risk cutting the process of development short by destroying sweatshop jobs, activists should instead buy products made in these factories and embrace the forces of economic development that will improve the lives of sweatshop workers. *New York Times* columnist Nicholas Kristof recently wrote that people need to rethink their objections to sweatshops and that "we need to build a constituency of humanitarians who view low-wage manufacturing as a solution."[7] I hope you will join this constituency by the time you are finished reading this book.

---

[7] Nicholas Kristof, "My Sweatshop Column," *New York Times*, January 14, 2009. Retrieved from http://kristof.blogs.nytimes.com/2009/01/14/my-sweatshop-column/.

2

The Anti-Sweatshop Movement

The modern anti-sweatshop movement began developing in the early 1990s, but much of the activity was limited to isolated protests and individual actions. In the latter half of the 1990s, the movement developed many interrelated organizations that waged sustained campaigns against sweatshops. Most of those organizations continue their anti-sweatshop activism today. The movement contains a mix of celebrities, politicians, unions, student activists, and scholars. Some affiliate with major anti-sweatshop organizations, whereas others speak out or protest on their own.

There are significant differences between the different organizations within the anti-sweatshop movement in terms of both the changes for which they advocate and how they pursue their advocacy. However, all of the major anti-sweatshop organizations have this in common: They all believe that free-market competition in the global economy is not, at least alone, the best way to improve the lives of sweatshop workers. The groups vary in their opinion of exactly how the process of free market competition should be altered to improve the lives of workers. Some advocate consumer activism through either boycotts or "shop with a conscience" programs. Other groups want legal mandates created and enforced that dictate living wages, health and safety standards, and working-hour regulations. Some groups favor trade restrictions on countries that do not mandate and enforce these labor standards. Some groups concern themselves only with child labor, whereas others focus mostly on the freedom to unionize.

The remainder of this chapter traces the development of the major players in the anti-sweatshop movement and outlines what reforms each group wants and how it agitates for them. No attempt is made within this chapter to assess the merits of the policies they advocate; these are examined later. Rather, this chapter provides a guide to how those later arguments apply to the individual organizations.

THE DEVELOPMENT OF THE ANTI-SWEATSHOP MOVEMENT

Although most of the modern anti-sweatshop movement has its beginnings in the 1990s, there were important predecessors. Unionization and activist campaigns for domestic sweatshops were active in the United States around the turn of the twentieth century. Most important for the modern international movement, however, was the creation of the International Labor Organization (ILO) in 1919, and it continues to play an important role in the anti-sweatshop movement today.

The ILO is an organization of governments, employers, and workers, and is now an agency of the United Nations. The ILO develops conventions that are legally binding on countries that enter into ILO treaties, as well as recommendations that serve as guidelines but are not legally binding. The ILO "core labor standards" conventions address the freedom of association and right to bargain collectively, the elimination of forced and compulsory labor, the abolition of child labor, and the elimination of discrimination in the workplace. The ILO's 1998 Declaration on Fundamental Principles and Rights at Work reiterated these principles; the ILO then launched a campaign to achieve universal ratification of the eight conventions in these areas.[1]

There are 180 additional conventions and 200 recommendations that cover many other aspects of employment. Approximately seventy of the conventions and recommendations deal with occupational safety and health standards.[2] According to the ILO, it places a "special importance on developing and applying a preventive safety and health culture in workplaces worldwide."[3]

ILO conventions also mandate members to set a minimum wage (conv. 131), limit maximum working hours to eight in a day and

---

[1] International Labor Organization, Declaration on Fundamental Principles and Rights at Work, retrieved from http://www.ilo.org/declaration/lang--en/index.htm.

[2] Retrieved from http://www.ilo.org/safework/info/standards-and-instruments/lang--en/index.htm.

[3] ILO, Safety and Health at Work, Retrieved from http://www.ilo.org/global/topics/safety-and-health-at-work/lang--en/index.htm.

forty-eight in a week (conv. 1), and guarantee paid maternity leave for fourteen weeks plus paid work breaks for breastfeeding (conv. 183). Conventions cover a host of other areas, as well.

Although ILO conventions are binding only on member countries that ratify them, the ILO also campaigns for more widespread acceptance of its conventions and recommendations. These conventions and recommendations have also served as focal points for many of the anti-sweatshop groups that developed in the 1990s.

The real birth of the modern international anti-sweatshop movement came in 1990. In Europe, the Clean Clothes Campaign began in the Netherlands. This coalition of consumer, labor, religious, human rights, and feminist groups agitated for better conditions in sweatshops. In the United States, the National Labor Committee (NLC) decided to make international sweatshops its signature campaign. The NLC's director, Charlie Kernaghan, one of the most influential early anti-sweatshop activists, gained notoriety for himself and the cause of sweatshops by going after prominent brands and celebrities with otherwise wholesome images in the media. In one famous instance, he confronted Kathy Lee Gifford on television with a Honduran garment worker who produced her line of clothes, and made Kathy Lee cry (see Chapter 4). NLC's activism helped raise awareness that would foster the creation of future anti-sweatshop groups.

The NLC primarily investigates and exposes what it believes to be human and labor rights abuses committed by U.S. companies producing goods in the Third World. It engages in research and popular campaigns to raise awareness in the United States about these abuses, and attempts to help workers abroad learn and defend what it believes are their rights. It has issued hundreds of reports alleging abusive sweatshop activities in dozens of countries. The NLC gives workers' efforts in these countries international visibility and "press[es] for international legal frameworks with effective enforcement mechanisms that will help create a space where fundamental internationally recognized worker rights can be assured."[4]

In addition to publicizing specific conditions, the NLC also pushes for legislation. For example, the NLC wrote the 2006 Decent Working

---

[4] Institute for Global Labour and Human Rights, Mission, retrieved from http://www. nlcnet.org/about.

Conditions and Fair Competition Act with Senator Byron Dorgan.[5] The bill, which failed to pass, would have prohibited the import, sale, or export of sweatshop goods. Goods made under conditions that violate the core ILO standards would have been banned.

American unions were vitally important in making international sweatshops a popular issue and getting other anti-sweatshop organizations started. Jeff Ballinger, who had headed the American Federation of Labor and Congress of Industrial Organization's (AFL-CIO) Jakarta office and organized Indonesian workers for nearly four years, began a public campaign against Nike when he returned to the United States in 1992. The publicity he generated helped encourage groups such as Global Exchange, the NLC, and the People of Faith Network to begin anti-Nike campaigns of their own. This anti-Nike campaign would also prove "most influential to the student movement" because so many schools had contracts with Nike.[6]

The AFL-CIO's anti-sweatshop activism has sometimes consisted of direct political lobbying, but much has taken the form of funding other anti-sweatshop groups. The AFL-CIO actively supported and lobbied for the Decent Working Conditions and Fair Competition Act. It claimed that the bill "offers a positive, proactive alternative to the current race to the bottom in the global sweatshop economy, one based on full respect for workers' human rights. Our goal is to create economic incentives for both corporations and governments to raise standards and protect workers' rights around the world." The AFL-CIO's own statements, however, give reason to question whether the welfare of Third World workers was really their motive. Their statement of support begins by describing how global competition is harming the U.S. economy, and their conclusion claims the legislation will be "a powerful vehicle ... to take back our economy."[7] The following chapter explores why the goals of helping sweatshop workers and "taking back our economy" are at odds with one another.

The AFL-CIO created the American Center for International Labor Solidarity in 1997 and continues to help fund and direct the

---

[5] Support Grows for Anti-Sweatshop Legislation, retrieved from http://www.nlcnet.org/alerts?id=0180.

[6] Featherstone and USAS, *Students Against Sweatshops* (New York: Verso, 2002), 8–9.

[7] Retrieved from http://www.aflcio.org/About/Exec-Council/EC-Statements/New-Tools-to-Fight-Sweatshop-Abuses.

center.[8] According to the center, "The programs implemented and the partners chosen are determined solely by the Solidarity Center and the AFL-CIO."[9] John Sweeney, AFL-CIO president emeritus, chairs the center's board, and all of the center's board members hold high-ranking positions in the AFL-CIO or other labor unions.[10]

The center's mission is to help "unions and community groups world-wide to achieve equitable, sustainable, democratic development and to help men and women everywhere stand up for their rights and improve their living and working conditions."[11] Specifically, the center claims that "strong trade unions must endeavor to ensure that workers are able to exercise their full spectrum of rights, including ILO core labor standards."[12] Furthermore, "All workers deserve decent jobs where they are treated with respect and dignity and paid a living wage."[13] The Solidarity Center also helps workers abroad fight for worker safety and health and assists workers in improving their conditions to meet international standards.[14]

The United Needle and Textile Workers Union (UNITE) was also active in publicizing sweatshop conditions. They probably received the most attention for their mid-1990s campaign against Guess Jeans, which got a popularity boost from the endorsement of the appropriately Luddite-named band Rage Against the Machine. As Featherstone and the United Students Against Sweatshops (USAS) note, "Such Campaigns reflected, in part, new AFL-CIO president John Sweeney's emphasis on corporate campaigns."[15]

The publicity that sweatshops were receiving created political pressure to do something about them. In 1996, the Clinton administration, in conjunction with a coalition of unions, apparel companies, and human rights groups, developed basic labor codes they wanted factories to

---

[8] Solidarity Center, About Us, retrieved from http://www.solidaritycenter.org/content.asp?pl=409&contentid=409.

[9] Ibid.

[10] Solidarity Center, Board of Trustees, retrieved from http://www.solidaritycenter.org/content.asp?pl=409&sl=409&contentid=515.

[11] Solidarity Center, About Us.

[12] Solidarity Center, Worker & Human Rights, retrieved from http://www.solidaritycenter.org/content.asp?pl=405&sl=405&contentid=420.

[13] Ibid.

[14] Solidarity Center, Safety & Health, retrieved from http://www.solidaritycenter.org/content.asp?pl=405&sl=405&contentid=418.

[15] Featherstone and USAS, *Students Against Sweatshops*, 9.

meet, and created the Fair Labor Association (FLA) to serve as the monitoring body and enforce the codes. Companies, universities, and individual suppliers can affiliate with the FLA. When a company or university affiliates, it must submit a list of their suppliers to be monitored by the FLA. The FLA's workplace code of conduct includes: no forced labor, child labor, workplace harassment, or discrimination; health and safety standards; freedom to bargain collectively; payment of local minimum wages or prevailing industry wages, whichever is higher; maximum hours of work; and overtime compensation.[16]

Companies that affiliate with the FLA commit to establishing internal systems to monitor working conditions, maintaining the code standards, and submitting to external monitoring from the FLA. Since 2003, the FLA has conducted more than 800 independent audits in factories supplying affiliates.[17] Results of the audits are published online, and affiliates are expected to work with suppliers to correct any violations. The FLA is funded by the fees paid by its affiliates. The more radical anti-sweatshop critics of the FLA argued that it amounted to "self-monitoring" and was "thoroughly controlled by manufacturers."[18] This helped lead to more activism, specifically the spread of the student anti-sweatshop movement, and an alternative monitoring organization.

After a few years of isolated and fragmented campus activities, in the spring of 1998, the USAS, a coalition of anti-sweatshop groups at universities across the United States, was formed. U.S. unions strongly supported the creation and growth of the student anti-sweatshop movement. In 1996, the AFL-CIO began a Union Summer program that placed college students in summer internships with unions. In this program, students began investigating their universities' connections to sweatshops. However, according to United Students Against Sweatshops:

The campus movement didn't begin in earnest until summer 1997, in UNITE's New York City offices. Ginny Coughlin, a newly hired UNITE organizer, asked UNITE's summer interns to research the connections between collegiate apparel and sweatshops for a possible campus campaign. That campaign, UNITE organizers reasoned, could complement the union's own anti-sweatshop efforts. Sensing that the FLA was helping manufacturers win the public relations battle, says Alan

---

[16] Retrieved from http://www.fairlabor.org/our-work/labor-standards.
[17] Retrieved from http://www.fairlabor.org/sites/default/files/sci-factsheet_7-23-12.pdf
[18] Featherstone and USAS, *Students Against Sweatshops*, 10.

Howard, then assistant to the president of UNITE, "the union, to its credit, said, 'Here's a very important base that can help us deal with this offensive.' "[19]

Tico Almeida, a Duke student and one of UNITE's interns, began an anti-sweatshop campaign when he returned to campus that fall. The students succeeded in convincing the university to pass a code that required "manufacturers of Duke apparel to maintain safe, independently monitored facilities where workers were free to organize."[20] This student victory helped inspire activists on other campuses and led to the creation of the USAS the following spring.

The USAS itself has noted that it "has built strong relationships with North American unions, which are, in turn, showing remarkable dedication to the new generation."[21] They also note that many students involved in the movement take jobs as union organizers both in the summer and after graduation. This is important because "turnover is one of student activism's biggest curses ... because there's no way to keep graduates involved," but "USAS's strong relationship with US unions is helping the organization build domestic solidarity" and avoid the disintegration of the movement after a few victories.[22] The AFL-CIO also helps fund the USAS. For instance, it donated $40,000 to the USAS in academic year 1999–2000 and another $50,000 the following academic year.[23]

Observers have noted that the USAS is "inseparably linked to the youthful, worldwide anti-corporate movement now visible at any display of conspicuous capitalism."[24] Their very broad and general concerns are evident from how they describe their own organization:

We envision a world in which society and human relationships are organized cooperatively, not competitively. We struggle towards a world in which all people live in freedom from oppression, in which people are valued as whole human beings rather than exploited in a quest for productivity and profits.

We struggle against racism, sexism, heterosexism, classism, ableism, and other forms of oppression within our society, within our organizations, and within ourselves. We strive to build relationships with other grassroots movements

---

[19] Featherstone and USAS, *Students Against Sweatshops*, 11.
[20] Featherstone and USAS, *Students Against Sweatshops*, 12.
[21] Featherstone and USAS, *Students Against Sweatshops*, 97.
[22] Ibid.
[23] Ibid.
[24] Featherstone and USAS, *Students Against Sweatshops*, 2.

because we believe the student-labor solidarity movement is part of a larger struggle for global justice.[25]

These sweeping generalizations allow a diverse body of students who are discontent with globalization to align themselves. As a result, views differ considerably within the USAS and between campus affiliates. In general, however, most of the USAS's anti-sweatshop activity has taken the form of affiliates opposing their own campus's use of sweatshop labor to produce college-licensed apparel. Students have held protests, sit-ins, and hunger strikes as well as taken over college presidents' offices to convince their colleges to adopt policies ensuring that their clothes are not made in sweatshops.

As student activism increased, more universities began joining the FLA. However, the USAS thought that the FLA failed to adequately monitor factories.[26] In response, they, in conjunction with scholars, labor unions, and human rights groups, created the Worker Rights Consortium (WRC) in 2001. This organization set the bar higher than the FLA did and focused on investigating worker complaints rather than certifying facilities as "sweat free." Much student activism became focused on convincing their colleges to abandon the FLA and join the WRC.

The WRC now has more than 175 college and university affiliates.[27] The WRC has developed a model code that requires university suppliers to pay a living wage and comply with the U.S. Occupational Safety and Health Administration's (OSHA) health and safety standards. Universities are encouraged, but not required, to adopt the model code when they affiliate with the WRC. The WRC will take colleges as members who have their own codes provided the codes protect workers in the areas of wages, hours of work and overtime compensation, freedom of association, workplace health and safety, women's rights, child labor, forced labor, harassment and abuse, nondiscrimination, and compliance with local laws.[28]

---

[25] USAS, About Us, retrieved from http://usas.org/about-us/.

[26] For a general account of the difficulties of monitoring working conditions, see Jill Esbenshade, *Monitoring Sweatshops: Workers, Consumers, and the Global Apparel Industry* (Philadelphia: Temple University Press, 2004).

[27] Worker Rights Consortium, Mission, retrieved from http://www.workersrights.org/about/.

[28] Worker Rights Consortium, Frequently Asked Questions, retrieved from http://www.workersrights.org/faq.asp.

When a college affiliates with the WRC, it must provide the organization with a list of all factories that produce goods with the college's logo and their locations. The WRC then monitors these factories and works to improve conditions when they do not live up to the college's code. Although the WRC does not recommend "cutting and running" as a first step when a supplier is out of compliance, it ultimately advocates ceasing to do business with the supplier if the latter continues refusing to live up to the code. In return for its monitoring, the WRC requires affiliates to pay $1,000 or 1 percent of licensing revenue, whichever is greater, annually. Approximately 45 percent of the WRC's revenue comes from these fees; the rest comes from grants.[29]

In response to anti-sweatshop activism, the Academic Consortium on International Trade (ACIT), a group of international trade economists and lawyers, circulated a letter to college presidents urging them not to take ill-informed actions in response to student activism.[30] The consortium warned that, among other things, pushing for higher wages could hurt workers by jeopardizing jobs that pay better than other alternatives.

In response to the ACIT's letter, Scholars Against Sweatshop Labor was created. Led by Robert Polin of the University of Massachusetts, the scholars drew up their own letter in late 2001 that was supportive of the student anti-sweatshop movement, the WRC and FLA, and the broad anti-sweatshop movement.[31] The letter was signed by 434 scholars, 73 percent of whom were economists. Although the letter recognized the merits of many points raised by the ACIT economists, it defended the monitoring organizations and disputed the evidence ACIT pointed to showing that wages in sweatshops were superior to other alternatives. Although they recognized the potentially negative economic consequences of mandating high wages or workplace conditions, they argued that there is "no reason to assume that a country or region that sets reasonable standards must experience job losses," and further claimed that higher retail prices could allow improved conditions without leading to job loss.[32] Overall, the letter gave scholarly

---

[29] Retrieved from http://www.workersrights.org/faq.asp.
[30] ACIT, Steering Committee, retrieved from http://www.fordschool.umich.edu/rsie/acit/Documents/July29SweatshopLetter.pdf.
[31] SASL, Statement October 2001, retrieved from http://www.peri.umass.edu/253/.
[32] Ibid.

credibility to the anti-sweatshop movement and helped student activists in their lobbying of universities.

Over the last twenty-plus years the anti-sweatshop movement transformed from a few individuals exposing working conditions to a large movement with many permanent, well-funded organizations with organized anti-sweatshop campaigns.

CONCLUSION

The anti-sweatshop movement is a diverse group of organizations with many different specific goals and strategies, but some common themes do arise. First, many but not all of these organizations have ties with First World unions. The next chapter argues that there are good economic reasons for these ties to exist. Although the specific details of the reforms for which individual organizations call may differ, most advocate for some form of a legal "living" minimum wage. Most want some government-set mandatory working conditions that include health and safety as well as regulations on working hours. Most are opposed to child labor. Most believe that, at a minimum, companies should respect and conform to local labor laws, and that these laws should become stronger. Most believe in some form of support for unionization of Third World workers. Where the groups seem to differ most is in whether they explicitly endorse trade sanctions when countries do not have regulations up to their standards or whether they will endorse boycotts when individual companies fail to live up to standards. All of these policies are analyzed in subsequent chapters.

The anti-sweatshop groups are obviously not the only interest groups involved in shaping national and global trade policy. Multinational firms and other exporters and importers also play an important role, as do the governments in Third World countries. The World Trade Organization has resisted most attempts to incorporate labor standards into trade agreements because of opposition from Third World countries.[33] This

---

[33] See Doug Irwin, *Free Trade Under Fire* (Princeton: Princeton University Press, 2002), 215–224 for a discussion of the politics surrounding the adoption of labor standards in trade agreements.

book is not concerned with the political forces that have given rise to the current status quo in international labor policy.[34] Instead, the focus is on whether Third World workers would benefit if the status quo changed in the direction many activists desire. The remainder of the book is thus concerned with the desirability of various political equilibria, not the forces that give rise to any particular political equilibrium.

APPENDIX: OTHER ANTI-SWEATSHOP GROUPS

This appendix contains brief descriptions of some of the other major anti-sweatshop groups that were not discussed in the main text of this chapter. Readers not interested in these details can skip to the next chapter without any loss of continuity in the book's argument.

International Labor Rights Forum

The International Labor Rights Forum (ILRF) was engaged in anti-sweatshop activism before an anti-sweatshop movement truly existed. The ILRF now runs campaigns targeting agricultural workers as well as traditional sweatshop workers. The organization promotes labor rights through public education, research, legislation, litigation, and collaboration with labor, government, and business groups.

One important aspect of the ILRF is its focus on including labor rights in U.S. and global trade agreements. In 1984, it helped get the first labor rights clause inserted into a trade agreement. This clause required any country seeking preferential access to U.S. markets to respect internationally recognized workers' rights, including freedom of association.[35] The organization also played a leading role in adoption of the ILO convention. More recently, the ILRF has been involved in lobbying for labor provisions in many free trade agreements

---

[34] For a book more focused on the political forces that shape the outcome of the sweatshop debate, see Shae Garwood, *Advocacy across Borders: NGOs, Anti-Sweatshop Activism, and the Global Garment Industry* (Sterling, VA: Kumarian Press, 2011).

[35] ILRF, Mission Statement, retrieved from http://www.laborrights.org/about-ilrf.

including NAFTA and DR-CAFTA, as well as with bilateral trade deals with Colombia and Panama.[36]

The ILRF claims that although free trade can promote development, "U.S. trade agreements can create harmful downward pressure in developing world labor markets if they do not include strong and enforceable labor rights mechanisms."[37] The ILRF believes that "as long as poor labor standards exist in one country, workers everywhere will be hurt."[38] As a result, it would prefer to incorporate such labor rights "social causes" into the World Trade Organization.[39] Thus far, it has been unsuccessful in that regard, and has settled for obtaining inclusion of provisions in individual trade agreements.

The ILRF also sponsors the "SweatFree Communities" campaign. The campaign, started in 2003, lobbies state and local governments to procure their uniforms, garments, and other apparel from factories that have been certified as "SweatFree." During the campaign's first 7 years, 9 states, 40 cities, 15 counties, and 118 school districts adopted their SweatFree policy.[40]

U.S. Labor Education in the Americas Project

The U.S. Labor Education in the Americas Project (USLEAP) is a nonprofit organization that promotes respect for the rights of workers in Latin America. It advocates for a global economy in which all workers are treated fairly, paid a living wage, and respected by corporations and governments. USLEAP's main contribution to the anti-sweatshop movement is its Sweatshop (Maquiladora Worker) Project, through which it works with a wide range of groups and unions including the International Textile, Garment, and Leather Workers Federation, the AFL-CIO's Solidarity Center, Maquila Solidarity Network, Sweatfree Communities, United Students Against Sweatshops, and the Workers Rights Consortium. USLEAP links North American codes of conduct,

---

[36] ILRF, Creating a Sweatfree World: Changing Global Trade Rules, retrieved from http://www.laborrights.org/creating-a-sweatfree-world/changing-global-trade-rules.

[37] Ibid.

[38] Ibid.

[39] Ibid.

[40] SweatFree Communities, About Us, retrieved from http://www.sweatfree.org/about_us.

monitoring, and student anti-sweatshop activities to specific campaigns in Central America and Mexico where it directly engages companies at the request of workers in the region.[41] Although technically an independent nonprofit organization, USLEAP's board tends to be dominated by officials from a variety of unions. Tim Beaty of the International Brotherhood of Teamsters is the vice chair of USLEAP, and ten of the sixteen USLEAP board members are union officials.[42]

Maquila Solidarity Network

The Maquila Solidarity Network was created in 1994 to work with women's and labor rights organizations in Mexico, Central America, and Asia. Similar to other groups, the Network advocates for a locally determined "living wage," and believes that governments should set and enforce regulations for decent working conditions.[43] Although it has many of the same objections to sweatshops as the other groups, and opposes the use of child labor, the Maquila Solidarity Network explicitly says that it does not advocate boycotting goods produced by child labor or calling for unilateral government action to impose trade sanctions on countries that use child labor.[44]

STITCH

STITCH is less of a public advocacy group than are many of the other organizations in the anti-sweatshop movement. In 1994, after attending a Guatemalan labor conference, a group of North American women decided to form a women's solidarity network, which resulted in the founding of STITCH in 1998. STITCH mainly supports the leadership capacity and skills of women workers in Latin America through

---

[41] USLEAP, Sweatshop (Maquiladora Worker) Project, retrieved from http://www. usleap.org/about-us/projects-and-initiatives/sweatshop-maquiladora-worker-project.

[42] USLEAP, Board of Directors, retrieved from http://www.usleap.org/about-us/board-directors.

[43] Maquila Solidarity Network, Questions about Sweatshops, retrieved from http://en. maquilasolidarity.org/FAQ/sweatshops?SESS89c5db41a82abcd7da7c9ac60e04ca5f= qadsupha9gfn9id09jdcqll090#9.

[44] Maquila Solidarity Network, Child Labour: Do's and Don'ts, retrieved from http://en. maquilasolidarity.org/node/662?SESS89c5db41a82abcd7da7c9ac60e04ca5f=qadsupha 9gfn9id09jdcqll090.

workshops, program exchanges, publications, and formation of alliances with them.[45]

Organizations Abroad

Although much of the anti-sweatshop movement is located in North America, a few European organizations are worth briefly examining. The Clean Clothes Campaign (CCC) was one of the earliest anti-sweatshop organizations. Based in the Netherlands, the CCC is an alliance of organizations in fifteen European countries with members including trade unions and NGOs. The organization educates and mobilizes consumers, lobbies companies and governments, and provides solidarity support to Third World workers.[46]

The CCC believes that governments should pass legislation that supports labor standards and sanctions those companies and governments that do not. It believes these standards should include the ILO's core labor standards as well as "the right to a living wage based on a regular working week that does not exceed 48 hours; humane working hours with no forced overtime; a safe and healthy workplace free from harassment; and a recognised employment relationship with labour and social protection."[47] Although it supports government regulation, the CCC does not support boycotts that put workers' jobs at risk.[48]

The UK-based War on Want has a "love fashion hate sweatshops" campaign. Similar to the CCC, it does not support boycotts, recognizing that they lead only to further job losses, but does support government regulation.[49] It claims, "Real change can only be achieved through government regulation that protects the rights of workers supplying UK companies." Specifically, it agitates for regulations that would

---

[45] STITCH, Who We Are and What We Do, retrieved from http://www.stitchonline.org/whowhat.asp.

[46] Clean Clothes Campaign, Who We Are, retrieved from http://www.cleanclothes.org/about.

[47] Clean Clothes Campaign, FAQs, What are ILO Conventions and Core Labour Standards, retrieved from http://www.cleanclothes.org/issues/faq/ilo.

[48] Clean Clothes Campaign, FAQs, retrieved from http://www.cleanclothes.org/issues/faq/boycotts.

[49] War on Want, Love Fashion Hate Sweatshops, retrieved from http://www.waronwant.org/campaigns/love-fashion-hate-sweatshops.

guarantee workers a living wage, decent working conditions, and the right to form a union.

Also based in the United Kingdom is a separate Students Against Sweatshops organization that demands an end to child labor, unsafe conditions, forced overtime, and harassment of female workers, and calls for a living wage, reasonable hours, independent trade unions, and safe working conditions.[50]

---

[50] Students Against Sweatshops, Stamp Out Sweatshops! Retrieved from http://www. studentsagainstsweatshops.org.uk/about.html.

3

The Economics of Sweatshop Wage Determination

Critics point out working conditions in sweatshops that any citizen in the developed world would find deplorable. The anti-sweatshop movement suggests many laws, regulations, and consumer activist tactics in the hope of improving the lives of sweatshop workers. Sentiments such as those expressed by Sheri Davis, a graduate student at Ohio State University and participant at a USAS rally, are common: "Everybody wants to have a living wage. Everybody wants to be able to take care of themselves and their family. Everybody wants to retire and feel good, enjoy life. Breathe. Live. Eat. You know, the regular shit. We're not asking for nothing extra special."[1] Unfortunately, wishing does not make it so.

Each law, regulation, or activist activity impacts the incentives of companies that hire sweatshop workers. Some of these actions may help sweatshop workers. Unfortunately, others will have unintended secondary consequences that impact employer incentives and, as a result, leave already poor sweatshop workers even worse off. Activists need to understand the market forces that determine wages to understand which policies can help workers and which will hurt them.

HOW ARE WAGES DETERMINED?

Wages and working conditions in sweatshops are set by the same process that sets wages and working conditions in wealthier countries: supply and demand. The wages and conditions are determined by bidding between employers and potential employees. Employers often

---

[1] Featherstone and USAS, *Students Against Sweatshops*, 39.

make the offer, but potential employees are free to accept the offer or reject it. If employers cannot attract enough workers at the wage they are offering, they will need to raise the wage to convince more workers to choose to work for them. But they will not continue raising their wage offers indefinitely.

A worker's productivity limits the maximum amount an employer is willing to pay them. Economists call this the worker's *marginal revenue product.* Simply put, an employee who generates $2.00 per hour of revenue for the employer that would not have been generated if that employee was not working there has a marginal revenue product of $2.00 per hour. The maximum wage an employer would be willing to pay that worker is $2.00 per hour. At a wage of $2.01 per hour, the employer is losing one cent for every hour that employee works. A profit-maximizing business does not hire workers who increase their losses.

However, just because a worker can create $2.00 per hour of revenue does not mean that an employer would like to pay them that much. Ideally, the employer would like to pay them nothing and pocket the entire $2.00 per hour as profit. But few people, even in very poor countries, are willing to work for nothing. To convince a worker to accept a job, the employer must offer them more than whatever that worker can make at what the worker perceives as their next best alternative. Workers compare the available wages, working conditions, hours, and so forth, and choose the offer that they think is in their best interest.

These two factors determine the bounds at which wage bargaining can occur. The upper bound is limited by the worker's productivity. The lower bound is limited by the worker's next best alternative. The actual wage must fall somewhere between these two bounds.

In practice, these bounds are often very close together. When an area contains more than one sweatshop, the amount of revenue a worker could generate by working at any one of them is closely related to the amount of revenue that they could generate in another sweatshop. If an employer offers workers wages far below their productivity, the employee can find another firm who would profit by offering them higher wages. For many workers, their next best alternative to working in one sweatshop is working in another. As a result, wages are bid up to approximately the worker's marginal productivity. In some situations, such as where factory jobs are few, the gap between productivity and the worker's next best alternative can be larger.

If activists want to help sweatshop workers, they need to advocate for things that will raise sweatshop workers' productivity and give them more alternatives. In short, policies need to raise these upper and lower bounds. Economists have found that approximately 70–80 percent of the variation in wages across nations can be attributed to differences in productivity.[2] Thus, the main focus of activists needs to be on raising the upper bound by increasing productivity. Advocating any policy to raise wages that does not raise these bounds risks raising workers' compensation above their productivity; thus, unemploying the workers that the activists were trying to help.

ECONOMIC IMPACT OF ACTIVISTS' ACTIONS

Anti-sweatshop activists are often unaware of the basic economics of wage determination. As a result, they advocate policies or pursue courses of action that harm sweatshop workers. Legal minimum or "living" wages are one such policy endorsed by many of the groups described in the previous chapter.

Passing a law that mandates higher pay does nothing to make workers more productive, nor does it create new alternatives to bid workers away from their current jobs. Legal minimum wages simply outlaw potential gains from trade between employers and workers. Paraphrasing liberal Nobel Laureate Paul Samuelson, it does a potential sweatshop worker – who can create $2.00 per hour of value – no good to know that by law he must be paid $3.00 per hour if that very law keeps him from getting a job.[3]

A legal minimum wage of only 1 cent per hour is unlikely to unemploy even the least skilled workers. But it would also have no effect because wages would be higher to begin with. In some instances, a minimum wage could fall between the upper and lower bounds for particular workers and, as a result, raise their wages without unemploying them. But any minimum wage likely to positively affect those few workers will almost certainly also raise the legal minimum above another, less-skilled,

---

[2] See Doug Irwin, *Free Trade Under Fire*, 210.

[3] Samuelson's quote was: "What good does it do a black youth to know that an employer must pay him $2 an hour if the fact that he must be paid that amount is what keeps him from getting a job?" *Economics*, 9th ed. (New York: McGraw-Hill, 1973), 393–394.

worker's productivity and thus result in them being laid off. These laid-off workers end up employed in less desirable alternatives.[4]

Skeptics may respond that they do not see much evidence of the minimum wage causing unemployment in the United States. In fact, studies do find evidence of minimum wage-related unemployment among U.S. workers, but the effect is usually on a small segment of society that is young, a racial minority, and lacks a high school education. The reason is simple. Minimum wage laws in the United States are set at rates that are low enough relative to productivity that they are well below most people's upper and lower bounds.[5] A high minimum wage relative to productivity, however, can have a major effect.

The first federal minimum wage law in the United States illustrates this. The Fair Labor Standards Act set the U.S. minimum wage at 25 cents per hour in 1938. At the time, the average wage in the United States was 62.7 cents per hour, so most workers were unaffected. However, the law also applied to Puerto Rico, a poorer, less developed U.S. territory.[6] Many workers in Puerto Rico were earning only 3–4 cents per hour. The result was massive business bankruptcy and high unemployment in Puerto Rico. Imposing minimum wages at rates similar to those we have in the United States today in Third World sweatshop-using countries would have similarly disastrous consequences.

Advocates for minimum wages in Third World countries would likely respond that they realize they cannot impose a minimum wage as high as the one in the United States. Instead, they advocate a lower one that is often based off some local cost of living. But that begs the question, "Why not mandate a higher wage?" If activists believe that mandating higher wages can result in workers earning more without unemploying others, and they care about the workers, why wouldn't they want a

---

[4] Another unfortunate outcome that results from legal minimum wages above market-clearing levels is that workers waste resources competing to be the ones who get the remaining jobs. For a classic reference, see Yoram Barzel, "A Theory of Rationing by Waiting," *Journal of Law and Economics* 17 (1974), 73–95.

[5] Another reason we don't see larger unemployment effects is that employers compensate by decreasing worker benefits on other margins. Hourly employees may find their hours cut, or restaurants that used to let employees have free meals may now charge for them, and so forth.

[6] On the 1938 minimum wage in Puerto Rico, see Simon Rottenberg, "Minimum Wages in Puerto Rico," *The Economics of Legal Minimum Wages*, ed. Rottenberg (Washington: American Enterprise Institute, 1981), 327–339.

higher minimum wage? Implicitly, those who push for "not-too-high" minimum wages recognize the unemployment impact a legal minimum wage can have. Unfortunately, even at very low levels, a minimum wage large enough to have any positive effect for a few workers will also unemploy others.

A critic might argue that companies that employ sweatshop workers, or those that subcontract to them, often make millions of dollars. Such companies are not going to close because of a low minimum wage that raises their cost a little bit. This objection ignores the fact that all economic decisions are made on the margin. Companies do not face only the decision of whether to stay in business or to close. They choose how much to produce and what mix of capital, low-skilled workers, and high-skilled workers to use. If a company is maximizing its profits, it employs each of these factors of production up until the point that the revenue from the last (marginal) unit of each of them equals its cost.

A minimum wage increases the relative cost of low-skilled labor compared to high-skilled labor and capital. Rather than passively accepting lower profits, a profit-maximizing company responds to a minimum wage law by decreasing the amount of low-skilled labor it uses and replacing it with higher-skilled workers and capital. In the context of sweatshops, this could take the form of firing some workers and replacing them with machines but keeping other workers. Alternatively, a firm could move from a less productive country to a more productive country. Both of these actions may help some workers, but will harm the least productive and poorest ones. Firms may also balance the increased pay with cuts to other forms of compensation such as health and safety conditions, compensations activists often advocate for regulations to improve. This topic will be discussed in Chapter 5.

Economists have done much empirical work studying the effects of minimum wage laws. People skeptical of the standard economic argument present here typically point to an infamous 1995 book by economists David Card and Alan Krueger that argued empirically that the negative employment impact of minimum wage laws were minimal to nonexistent.[7] Economists have found problems with Card and

---

[7] David Card and Alan Krueger, *Myth and Measurement: The New Economics of the Minimum Wage* (Princeton: Princeton University Press, 1995).

Krueger's study, and much empirical work has been done since their analysis. Economists Kevin Murphy, Riche Deere, and Finis Welch summarized the problem with generalizing from Card and Kruger's analysis:

Each of the four studies examines a different piece of the minimum wage/ employment relationship. Three of them consider a single state, and two of them look at only a handful of firms in one industry. From these isolated findings Card and Krueger paint a big picture wherein increased minimum wages do not decrease, and may increase, employment. Our view is that there is something wrong with this picture. Artificial increases in the price of unskilled laborers inevitably lead to their reduced employment; the conventional wisdom remains intact.[8]

In the nearly twenty years since Card and Kruger's study, the vast majority of empirical studies have found that the minimum wage does lower employment. Economists David Neumark and William Wascher survey the vast literature studying the effect of the minimum wage in their recent book.[9] They find that the bulk of the empirical evidence accumulated over the last twenty years indicates that the minimum wage reduces employment for the least-skilled workers and lowers their earnings. In short, the Card and Kruger study is an outlier, not the norm.

A recent empirical study on the effect of the minimum wage in Indonesia is the most relevant study for sweatshops. In response to anti-sweatshop activism and the U.S. government's threat to remove special tariff privileges if human rights issues were not addressed, the Indonesian government made increasing the minimum wage a central component of its labor market policies in the 1990s. The real value of the minimum wage more than doubled between 1989 and 1996. What happened to manufacturing employment? Ann Harrison and Jason Scorse estimated that a 100-percentage point increase in Indonesia's minimum wage was associated with a decrease in employment between 12 and 36 percent. They also found that wage increases led to plant closures among small exporters. They conclude that "the significant negative impact on employment needs to be seriously considered in

---

[8] Donald Riche Deere, Kevin Murphy, and Finis Welch, "Sense and Nonsense on the Minimum Wage," *Regulation* 18 (1995), 47–56.

[9] David Neumark and William Wascher, *Minimum Wages* (Cambridge, MA: MIT Press, 2008).

any campaign to increase the mandated minimum wage or to increase compliance with the minimum wages."[10]

Activists also use boycotts to attempt to improve pay and working conditions in sweatshops. Their logic is straightforward. If consumers voluntarily cease purchasing products, or activists can persuade stores to stop stocking products that were made by workers who did not have high enough wages or safe enough working conditions, then companies will improve pay and conditions so that they can sell their products. Unfortunately, activists miss the secondary consequences of a boycott that end up harming workers. If a boycott is successful in raising wages or improving working conditions, that does not mean that some workers were not harmed. The relative cost of low-skilled labor compared to capital and higher-skilled workers will have increased with no actual improvement in worker productivity. As a result, the long-run effect of the boycott, similar to a minimum wage, will be to improve the lives of some relatively more-productive workers and throw the less-productive workers into worse alternatives. But boycotts are even worse than that.

In the short run, while a boycott is in effect, demand for the products made in sweatshops is lower, which means a lower demand for sweatshop workers. As a result, some workers are laid off, and in some cases orders dry up and factories temporarily close. Furthermore, a boycott decreases the upper bound of compensation because it impacts the amount of revenue an employee can create. When a boycott lowers the demand for a good, firms must cut prices to clear the market. But lower prices for the final good mean that the same effort and physical productivity on the part of a worker results in less revenue for the company. As a result, workers' marginal revenue product decreases through absolutely no fault of the employee. That means that the upper bound a firm is willing to pay an employee falls, and workers are harmed. Thus, boycotts harm workers while they are in effect. Even when boycotts are successful at achieving their objective, they harm some workers while helping others.

---

[10] Ann Harrison and Jason Scorse, "Multinationals and Anti-Sweatshop Activism," *American Economic Review* 100 (2010), 263. Curiously, Harrison and Scorse go to great lengths to cast anti-sweatshop activism in the most favorable light. Most of the paper emphasizes how they do not find any additional unemployment effects from anti-sweatshop activism beyond the unemployment effect of the minimum wage. But it is anti-sweatshop activism that was in large part responsible for increasing the minimum wage.

Economists Kimberly Elliot and Richard Freeman analyze how companies can respond to sweatshop activism.[11] Using survey data, they estimate that firms face a kinked demand for their products in which consumers are not very price sensitive when firms are exposed for having bad conditions. Yet these same consumers are price sensitive when good conditions are used as a marketing strategy. In other words, firms could lose a lot if their products are identified as being made under bad conditions, but they gain little from having them identified as being made under good conditions, compared to a baseline where consumers know nothing about the conditions. This means there is little scope for many companies to improve conditions from an uninformed baseline as a marketing strategy, but that firms may respond by improving conditions when they encounter negative publicity from anti-sweatshop activists. However, this does nothing to undermine the previous analysis. Whether companies improve conditions, ignore the activists, or have to cease production in response to consumer activism depends on the relative changes of the costs of improved conditions and revenue at stake. Which way a firm chooses is not a matter of a priori theory. However, even when firms choose to improve conditions, so long as those improved conditions are not a fixed cost, it will change the price of labor relative to other inputs and result in the firm employing fewer workers and throwing some workers into less desirable alternatives. Ultimately, Elliot and Freeman do not think direct activism to convince companies to voluntarily improve policies has been very successful, noting, "So far, however, the successes are ad hoc and often temporary."[12]

Trade sanctions and embargos have consequences similar to those of boycotts, but there are important differences. When activists push for trade sanctions against countries with lower wages or worse working conditions, they are advocating for a government policy that prohibits, or makes it more difficult, for everyone who might want to purchase the products made in sweatshops to do so. With a boycott, only the voluntary actions of some potential consumers decrease demand; others are

[11] Kimberly Elliot and Richard Freeman, "White Hats or Don Quixotes? Human Rights Vigilantes in the Global Economy," in *Emerging Labor Market Institutions for the Twenty First Century*, eds. R. Freeman et al. (Chicago: University of Chicago, 2004).

[12] Elliott and Freeman, "White Hats or Don Quixotes?" 86.

still free to buy. Thus, trade sanctions can lead to a bigger decrease in demand for sweatshop goods than boycotts, and often harm workers even more.

Trade sanctions are often aimed at changing government policies in poorer countries, whereas boycotts are aimed at convincing companies to change their policies. If trade sanctions are effective, governments create new laws mandating minimum wages or working condition standards that affect many firms. Unfortunately, this means that many more Third World workers are harmed if the trade sanction causes a change in government policy compared to a boycott because the higher-mandated compensation will affect many firms rather than just the one targeted by a boycott. If a trade sanction is not effective at convincing a government to change its policies, as is often the case, the sanction tends to remain in place for an extended period of time, resulting in a long-term decrease in demand for products made in these countries and thus harming workers. Sometimes, even when it becomes obvious to nearly everyone that a trade sanction is not going to cause another country to change its policies and the sanction harms poor people in the country, the sanction remains.[13] Witness the United States' fifty-plus-year embargo against Cuba.

When activists call for minimum wages, boycotts against firms with low wages or poor working conditions, or trade sanctions against countries with sweatshops they are taking actions that will harm many of the very workers they are intending to help. Many of these activists argue for such policies because they are simply ignorant of the basic economics of how sweatshop wages are determined and how their favored policies would interact with market forces. However, not all critics of sweatshops are so ignorant.

UNIONS AND SWEATSHOPS

A union's job is to bargain with employers to secure better wages and working conditions for union members. Why then have so many unions

---

[13] Kimberly Elliott, Gary Hufbauer, and Barbara Oegg report that since 1970, only one out of five times the United States has unilaterally imposed trade sanctions have they succeeded in achieving their objective. "Sanctions," in *The Concise Encyclopedia of Economics*, ed. David Henderson (2008), retrieved from http://econlib.org/library/Enc/Sanctions.html.

taken up the cause of Third World sweatshop workers? Most of these workers are not union members. However, the AFL-CIO, UNITE, and other union-funded organizations have argued for laws, regulations, or trade restrictions, supposedly to improve conditions for these workers.

The unions would have us believe that they are advocates for labor generally and they are helping Third World workers out of solidarity. But union members pay dues to benefit themselves, not for charity. The reality is that unions use the mantra of "helping sweatshop workers" to improve wages and working conditions for their much wealthier First World union members.

Unions understand the economics of wage determination. They understand that if one raises the cost of unskilled labor in Asia and Central America by mandating minimum wages or costly health and safety benefits, employers will demand a smaller quantity of that labor. What will they replace it with? Sometimes machines, but another substitute for low-cost, low-productivity labor is high-cost, high-productivity labor. When fewer garments are sewn in Honduras, more will be sewn in the United States by workers who are members of UNITE and other unions. The greater employer demand for U.S. garment workers helps unions increase their membership and bargain for higher wages and better working conditions for their members.

The protectionist nature of the anti-sweatshop movement is lost on many activists. Sue Casey, a USAS activist, reported an "uncomfortable moment when a UNITE official, presenting USAS with an award, thanked the student organization 'for helping us in our struggle *against imports.*' Because USAS goes out of its way not to take protectionist positions, Casy says, 'that really stunk' " (emphasis original).[14] Similarly, Tico Almeida, the student who helped start the student anti-sweatshop movement at Duke, laments, "Some media would later use the union relationship as 'proof' that the student anti-sweatshop movement had protectionist intentions, but a 'Made in the USA' provision – whether in corporate or university codes of conduct – has never once been proposed by the students."[15] "Made in the U.S.A." requirements or explicit intentions are not necessary to make USAS's actions result in

---

[14] Featherstone and USAS, *Students Against Sweatshops*, 17.
[15] Featherstone and USAS, *Students Against Sweatshops*, 16.

protectionist outcomes. As outlined in Chapter 2, USAS lobbies colleges to join the Worker Rights Consortium, which requires codes that mandate, among other things, creating their own minimum wages and following local minimum wage laws. The effect of these actions is to drive garment production from the Third World to the First World. Regardless of intent, the economic incentives created by USAS actions create protectionist outcomes that benefit the unions.

The "Shop with a Conscience Consumer Guide" provides a graphic illustration of how a seemingly non-protectionist-motivated policy generates a protectionist result. The International Labor Rights Forum, SweatFree Communities, and Sweatshop Watch jointly sponsor the guide, which lists firms selling products that have been made in factories the guide has deemed "sweat free." These sweat-free sources are either unionized or run as worker cooperatives, have healthy and safe working conditions, offer wages and benefits that will "lift workers' families out of poverty," and treat the workers with "respect, dignity, and justice."[16] So far, forty-one factories have met these criteria and been certified. As Figure 3.1 illustrates, twenty-nine of these factories are located in the United States and Canada; only eleven are located in Latin and South America; and a single factory is in Asia. Although consumers might feel they are "shopping with a conscience," they are mostly buying products made by wealthy First World union workers, decreasing the demand for products made in poorer countries and harming the employment prospects of the poorer Third World workers.

The unions masquerade publicly as friends to sweatshop workers, but the reality is much more devious. They intentionally advocate policies that will harm those very workers, and naïve young activists end up acting as tools to help the unions achieve their protectionist goals.[17] As economist David Henderson says, "Someone who intentionally gets you

---

[16] SweatFree Communities, Our Criteria, http://www.sweatfree.org/shopping_supplier criteria.

[17] This is not unlike the motives for the labor regulation passed during the progressive era in the United States. Economist Thomas Leonard argues that labor legislation with the public rationale of helping women or children was really the desire to limit their labor-force participation so that they would not compete with males. See, for example, "Protecting Family and Race: The Progressive Case for Regulating Women's Work," *American Journal of Economics and Sociology* 64(3): (2005), 757–791.

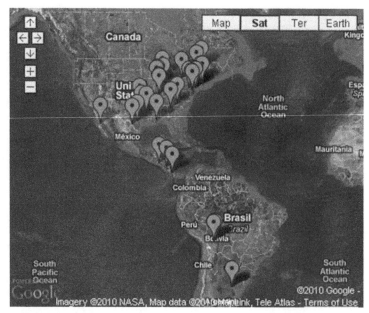

Figure 3.1 Location of factories supplying the Shop with a Conscience Guide
(one in Thailand not shown).

fired is not your friend."[18] Contrary to their claims, First World unions
are no friends of sweatshop workers.

AN ILLUSTRATION OF ECONOMICS IN ACTION: THE
BJ&B CAMPAIGN

The BJ&B factory, owned by the Korean firm Yupoong and located
in the Villa Altagracia export-processing zone in the Dominican
Republic, was a major producer of baseball hats for Nike, Reebok,
the Gap, and other major companies.[19] It employed more than 2,000
workers in 2001, but under harsh conditions. Workers were agitating
for a union, and UNITE helped them gain publicity and allies with the

---

[18] David R. Henderson, "The Case for Sweatshops," Hoover Institution, Stanford University,
February 7, 2000, retrieved from http://www.hoover.org/news/daily-report/24617.

[19] Unless otherwise cited, the facts in this section are from Shae Garwood, *Advocacy
across Borders: NGOs, Anti-Sweatshop Activism, and the Global Garment Industry*
(Sterling, VA: Kumarian Press, 2011), 180–185.

USAS. The FLA and WRC conducted audits and issued reports. The publicity eventually forced BJ&B to recognize the union in 2003, and enter into an agreement that would "give workers a 10 percent wage increase, educational scholarships, paid holidays, and the establishment of a workers' committee to deal with health and safety concerns at the factory."[20] The agreement was "hailed by many as a sign of the success of transnational organizing, particularly the strategic role played by USAS in exerting pressure on universities to take action through the WRC."[21]

The activists' victory was short lived. Soon the economic forces described above began asserting themselves. Yupoong threatened to close the factory and shift its production to overseas plants when the agreement was renegotiated just a year later in 2004. Activists again pressured the factory to negotiate and it stayed open, but it began laying off workers. Finally, in 2007, Yupoong closed the BJ&B plant because it was no longer competitive. The plant closure was really just the final nail in the coffin for the workers. The work force had already shrunk from 2,000 before activists pressured the factory to only 234 at the time of its closure.

Today, the location of the BJ&B factory is the site of one of the anti-sweatshop movement's latest "success" stories, the Altagracia Project. The Altagracia Project, founded in 2010, "was set up to operate as a model factory, showcasing that a factory could pay a living wage (three times the average wage for garment workers in the region), respect workers' rights to join a union, and at the same time turn a profit."[22] Thus far, the factory has been successful in selling its products at more than 600 college campuses throughout the United States.[23] It remains to be seen if the factory will be profitable in the long-run. It may have a sustainable "ethical branding" business model, which will be discussed in Chapter 10. However, even if it does stay in business, it is hard to judge the net effect of activist activity in the Villa Altagracia region as anything other than a horrible failure. BJ&B provided the best available

---

[20] Garwood, *Advocacy across Borders*, 181.

[21] Ibid.

[22] Garwood, *Advocacy across Borders*, 185.

[23] Alta Gracia, "What is a Living Wage?" Retrieved from http://altagraciaapparel.com/story.

alternative for 2,000 people a little over a decade ago. Activists' actions raised the cost of labor and caused the loss of all of the workers' jobs. The Altagracia Project employed only 120 people a decade later.

The laws of economics are clear. When the cost of labor increases, companies use less of it. Even these supposed "success stories" of the anti-sweatshop movement are not immune from these forces, and activists' actions ultimately made the vast majority of effected workers worse off.

SCHOLARLY OBJECTIONS TO SWEATSHOPS

Not all of the people who oppose sweatshops but understand the basic economic logic of wage determination are union demagogues. A growing scholarly literature challenges whether that logic can be applied accurately to Third World sweatshops.[24] Scholars have challenged whether the background conditions that are necessary to make trade mutually beneficial are present in Third World countries. They have also attempted to identify economic mechanisms that would allow wages to be increased without causing unemployment. The remainder of the chapter considers, and ultimately rejects, their arguments.

---

[24] Notable examples in this literature include: Denis G. Arnold and Norman E. Bowie, "Sweatshops and Respect for Persons," *Business Ethics Quarterly* 13 No. 2 (2003), 238; Denis Arnold and Laura Hartman, "Moral Imagination and the Future of Sweatshops," *Business and Society Review* 108 No. 4 (2003), 427. Denis Arnold, "Philosophical Foundations: Moral Reasoning, Human Rights, and Global Labor Practices," *Rising above Sweatshops: Innovative Approaches to Global Labor Challenges*, eds. Laura Hartman, Denis Arnold and Richard E. Wokutch (Westport, CT: Praeger, 2003), 79; John Miller, "Why Economists Are Wrong about Sweatshops and the Anti-Sweatshop Movement," *Challenge*, January/February (2003), 97; Robert Pollin, Justine Burns, and James Heintz, "Global Apparel Production and Sweatshop Labor: Can Raising Retail Prices Finance Living Wages?" *Cambridge Journal of Economics* 28, No. 2 (2004), 153–171; Denis Arnold and Laura Hartman, "Beyond Sweatshops: Positive Deviancy and Global Labour Practices," *Business Ethics: A European Review* 14, No. 3 (2005), 208; Denis Arnold and Laura Hartman, "Worker Rights and Low Wage Industrialization: How to Avoid Sweatshops," *Human Rights Quarterly* 28, No. 3 (2006), 676–700; Denis G. Arnold and Norman E. Bowie, "Respect for Workers in Global Supply Chains: Advancing the Debate over Sweatshops," *Business Ethics Quarterly* 17, No. 1 (2007), 139; and Denis Arnold, "Working Conditions: Safety and Sweatshops," in *The Oxford Handbook of Business Ethics*, eds. George Brenkert and Tom Beauchamp (New York: Oxford University Press, 2010), 635.

THE NECESSITY OF COMPETITIVE MARKETS

The most basic point made by defenders of sweatshops is that workers' voluntary choice to accept sweatshop employment demonstrates that sweatshops are the best alternative available to them. Therefore, activists should not advocate policies that could jeopardize these jobs. Critics have challenged whether this choice does demonstrate that sweatshops provide the best jobs, and whether conditions and wages cannot be improved without jeopardizing the jobs, on the grounds that the underlying conditions are not the type of competitive markets described in economics textbooks. Arnold and Hartman argue:

Free markets ... generate many benefits; but their ability to generate those benefits presumes certain fixed conditions. For example, transactions among workers and employers optimally satisfy the interests of each only if there is a free flow of information, the transaction is truly voluntary, people are able to make rational decisions about their self-interest, and there are many buyers and sellers (e.g. no potential for exploitative monopoly exists).[25]

Let us examine each of these conditions. The free flow of information improves economic efficiency. But information itself is not free. When Arnold and Hartman elaborate, they write that workers "may not be able to make a fully informed choice because of their lack of information about what lies ahead. Furthermore such labor choices, once made, can be difficult to undo when additional information is learned 'on the job.' "[26] This is a fact of life in all markets: It is always impossible to know what lies ahead, and there are often transaction costs for reversing course once new information is obtained.

Arnold and Hartman are holding up an unreasonable standard of "perfect competition" that never exists in any real world market and that assumes away the very problems the market must solve. Only in the end state of perfect competition is all information fully known. The real competitive market process is about discovering opportunities for gains from trade. Bidding by buyers and sellers reveals information about people's willingness to supply and demand all products, including labor. This very market process discovers the previously unknown

---

[25] Arnold and Hartman, "Beyond Sweatshops," 208.
[26] Arnold and Hartman, "Beyond Sweatshops," 209.

knowledge.[27] Rather than a flaw of markets, the lack of perfect information is one of the essential reasons we need markets.

Cases of outright fraud – in which employers intentionally disclose false information to employees – are more complicated. If the transaction cost of changing jobs is low, and the fraud easy to detect once one is on a job, then the market can sort the situation out easily, and the workers we observe still on the job are demonstrating that it is their best alternative. For example, job risks account for one-third of manufacturing quit rates in the United States.[28] The same process can work in sweatshops if employees find themselves in jobs that are riskier to their health and safety than was advertised to them.

In cases where transaction costs are high and the fraud is not easy to detect, the market would have a harder time sorting it out. Even in this case, however, in the long run, information from disgruntled workers can spread, help others make better choices, and even eliminate the harmful business practice by making it unprofitable because of the negative impact on the firm's reputation.

As a general rule, outright fraud should be illegal. In practice, identifying harmful fraud can be difficult. In some cases, government-mandated wages or working conditions may push total compensation above the level at which employers can profitably employ workers. In such a situation, advertising conditions that comply with the law, when the de facto conditions do not, may be beneficial for employees. I discuss the case for violating labor laws in Chapter 5. There is also a gray area around failure to disclose information compared to outright misrepresentation of it. Here it would depend on what local implicit custom surrounding contracts is, which can vary considerably between countries. Things that U.S. workers might expect to be disclosed workers in poorer countries might not expect. For example, disclosure of working with a chemical that causes cancer in seventy year olds might be expected in the United States but not in a country where the life expectancy is only fifty years. As I argue in Chapter 5, in many instances, providing poor working conditions is better for workers than mandating

---

[27] See Friedrich Hayek, "The Use of Knowledge in Society," *American Economic Review* 35, No. 4 (1945), 519–530.

[28] Kip Viscusi, Joseph Harrington, and John Vernon, *Economics of Regulation and Antitrust*, 4th ed. (Cambridge, MA: MIT Press, 2005), 836.

better conditions. Some may argue that workers have a "right" to better conditions, but the ability of workers to waive their "right" to better conditions is important for their own well-being. Whether that waiver comes after disclosure or with the norm of nondisclosure is of secondary importance.

Defenders of sweatshops assume that transactions are voluntary. John Miller has written that although sweatshop employment may be superior to the informal sector, this does not "suggest that these exchanges between employers and poor workers with few alternatives are in reality voluntary. ... Rather, these exchanges should be seen as 'trades of last resort' or 'desperate' exchanges that need to be protected by labor legislation regulating such things as limits on hours, a wage floor, and guaranteed health and safety requirements."[29] Arnold and Hartman, like Miller, write that preconditions for efficient markets are not met because "workers may agree to labour under poor conditions, but only because they have no other option for securing income."[30] Their objections relate to what economist Michael Munger has termed "euvoluntary exchange," or truly voluntary exchange. Munger argues for an exchange to be truly voluntary, there must be: (1) conventional ownership of items by both parties; (2) conventional capacity to transfer and assign this ownership to the other party; (3) the absence of regret, for both parties, after the exchange; (4) neither party is forced by a threat; and (5) neither party is coerced in the sense of being harmed by failing to exchange. It is point number five that Arnold, Hartman, and Miller are saying is absent in sweatshops, and thus the exchange is not truly voluntary. As Chapter 4 argues, the alternatives to sweatshop employment are often much worse and, as a result, workers feel like they must take offers of sweatshop employment. But Munger does not go wrong where these sweatshop critics do. He explains:

Exchanges that are not euvoluntary are generally welfare improving, and they improve the welfare of the least well off most of all. The confusion that arises in judging exchanges that are not euvoluntary is understandable, but unfortunate. The observer, seeing the degree of inequality, or desperation of one of the parties to a potential exchange, is actually perceiving a disparity in levels of welfare of the respective BATNAs, or "Best Alternatives to a Negotiated

---

[29] Miller, "Why Economists Are Wrong," 101.
[30] Arnold and Hartman, "Beyond Sweatshops," 209.

Exchange" [next best alternatives to trading]. This disparity is a consequence of differences that come before exchange is contemplated, and are not caused by the exchange.

But the confused observer seeks to help the less well off party by outlawing the exchange. The observer, believing that the party should not have to exchange on such terms, blunders in and dictates that the party should not be allowed to exchange on such terms. The problem is that this ensures that party is marooned at his grossly inferior BATNA, an outcome that access to exchange could have avoided.[31]

Lacking other good options does not change the fact that choosing the sweatshop job demonstrates that it is the worker's best alternative. True coercion takes away options by restricting the worker's choice set. Adding the option of working in a sweatshop expands the choice set. Adding governmental restrictions on what employers can offer workers, as Miller advocates, uses the threat of government coercion to take away some options, and that can throw workers into worse alternatives.

I do not assume that all people are always some version of a neo-classical "*homo economicus.*" People tend to choose what is in their best self-interest. It is impossible for outside observers to know the subjective tradeoffs made by other human beings.[32] Sweatshop workers have much more local knowledge of their particulars of time and place than First World scholars and activists do, and those workers certainly have the incentive to choose what is best for themselves.[33] I know of no systematic reason why their rationality should be questioned.

Arnold has also written that defenders of sweatshops "assume that multinational corporations always act with instrumental practical reason aimed at self-interested profit maximization. Such a view is empirically inaccurate."[34] Unfortunately, he merely asserts that the view is empirically inaccurate; he does not offer any proof. A corporation's job is to maximize shareholder value, and this includes the present value of the future stream of profits – not just short-run profits. Thus,

---

[31] Michael Munger, "Euvoluntary or Not, Exchange Is Just," *Social Philosophy and Policy* 28, No. 2 (2011), 211.

[32] See Edward Stringham, "Economic Value and Costs Are Subjective," *Handbook on Contemporary Austrian Economics*, ed. Peter Boettke (Cheltenham, UK: Edward Elgar, 2010), 43–66.

[33] A point recognized by Arnold himself in his discussion of moral imagination. See Arnold, "Philosophical Foundations," 79.

[34] Arnold, "Working Conditions," 637.

profit maximization leaves plenty of room for ethical branding or other sweatshop improvement policies that may decrease short-run profits but enhance long-run profitability through brand image. Citations of companies pursuing such policies do nothing to undermine the general profit maximization model.

This does not mean that companies have discovered all possible ways to maximize long-run profits. Competition is itself a discovery procedure.[35] When Arnold and Hartman document voluntary innovations that companies have made in worker health and safety, they perform a valuable service that is part of the market's discovery process.[36] But just because not every innovation has been discovered by the market process does not make corporations any less rational.

Finally, Arnold and Hartman question whether markets are beneficial if the number of buyers and sellers is small. In fact, elsewhere Arnold specifically singles me out: "Defenders of sweatshops such as Matt Zwolinski and Benjamin Powell, assume that such labor markets are competitive, but it is not clear that such an assumption is warranted. In many nations employers have monopsony power over the workers."[37] But many buyers and sellers need not be present for markets to produce efficient results.

If there is freedom of entry, a monopoly (monopsony) can produce results identical to a competitive market. If employers systematically pay workers less than their marginal revenue product, then new firms have an incentive to enter the market and bid the workers away from the underpaying firm because in the process, they will earn above-normal profits. As a result, even a single firm, when threatened with entry by other firms, pushes wages toward workers' marginal contribution to revenue.[38]

What if freedom of entry does not exist? Countries with sweatshops often suffer from numerous government regulations and interventions

---

[35] See Freidrich Hayek, "Competition as a Discovery Procedure," in *New Studies in Philosophy, Politics, Economics, and the History of Ideas* (Chicago: University of Chicago Press, 1978).

[36] Benjamin Powell, "In Reply to Sweatshop Sophistries," *Human Rights Quarterly* 28, No. 4 (2006), 1031–1042, praises Arnold and Hartman on exactly this point.

[37] Arnold, "Working Conditions," 651.

[38] Economists refer to this as contestable markets theory. There is also a large experimental economics literature that shows small numbers of buyers and sellers achieve results that approximate what a perfectly competitive market is supposed to achieve.

into the market. Even if a government regulation prohibits or raises the cost of entry, an individual sweatshop is better than none at all. If the single sweatshop disappeared, the labor market would be restricted even more. Rather than protest the sweatshop, inefficient regulations that inhibit the market process should be opposed.

Arnold and Hartman have mistaken sufficient conditions to ensure competitive markets generate beneficial results for necessary conditions. As economist Peter Boettke explains, "The 'invisible hand' solution does not emerge because the mainline economist postulates a perfectly rational individual interacting with other perfectly rational individuals within a perfectly structured market, as many critics suppose."[39] Instead, the beneficial outcomes generated by the invisible hand process emerge "through the reconciliation process of exchange within specific institutional environments. It is the 'higgling and bargaining' within the market economy, as Adam Smith argued, that produces social order."[40]

EFFICIENCY WAGES

Some scholars argue that the existence of efficiency wages means that firms can raise wages without unemploying workers. An *efficiency wage* is an above-market-rate wage paid to employees in order to induce greater productivity from the employees. Arnold and Hartman write, "There is evidence to support the claim that positive MNC deviants who voluntarily pay employees a living wage (or a 'fair wage') will achieve increases in worker productivity and loyalty. The most obvious ways in which wages affect productivity are captured by nutrition models of efficiency wages."[41] But nutritional needs cannot justify efficiency wages from profit-maximizing firms.

Malnourished workers are less productive, so employers should want to pay enough to ensure productivity. Arnold and Hartman state that because workers will spend income on other family members, firms may need to pay a worker two to four times the amount necessary

[39] Peter Boettke, *Living Economics: Yesterday, Today, and Tomorrow* (Oakland: The Independent Institute, 2012), xvii.
[40] Ibid.
[41] Arnold and Hartman, "Beyond Sweatshops," 217.

to meet the worker's minimum daily caloric intake. The increased productivity from an efficient diet may not offset the increased cost of paying two to four times the cost of that diet, however. More importantly, when the difference between malnourished and healthy worker productivity does justify paying enough to ensure a minimum caloric intake, firms can more efficiently provide those calories through free or subsidized meals at work. Although Arnold and Hartman grant that this is a possibility, it is, in fact, the norm.[42] An efficiency wage is rarely necessary to improve caloric intake because workers will spend some portion of their earnings on things other than their own food; thus, employers can almost always provide the calories directly at a lower cost.[43]

Arnold and Hartman also claim that "a second economic model [of efficiency wages] emphasizes the gift-exchange nature of employment relations, as opposed to the pure market exchange of such relations. On this model, employees who are compensated at rates significantly higher than the wages demanded by the market are seen as making a gift to workers, who reciprocate with greater productivity and greater loyalty."[44] A gift exchange-style efficiency wage may be necessary when the labor market is tight and monitoring employee productivity is difficult. If a firm pays an above-market wage in these cases, the employees have something to lose if they are caught underperforming, and they will work harder. Monitoring employee productivity is simple in most sweatshop jobs, and most such jobs exist in labor markets that have substantial unemployment or underemployment. Absent these two key characteristics, Arnold and Hartman are wrong to assume that an employee will work harder because higher wages are seen as a "gift" from the employer. Employees already work as hard as they are going to because labor market alternatives are poor and monitoring of workers is intense.

Efficiency wages may sometimes be necessary to maximize profits. However, the conditions necessary for efficiency wages to improve productivity are not widespread in Third World sweatshops. When

---

[42] Arnold and Hartman, "Worker Rights," 46.

[43] See Benjamin Powell and Ryan Murphy, "Nutritional Efficiency Wages and Unemployment: Where's the Beef?" Mimeo, 2013 for an extended formal analysis of this point.

[44] Arnold and Hartman, "Beyond Sweatshops," 218.

they are present, managers have every incentive to adopt them voluntarily. There is no reason to believe that pushing for higher wages will result in higher productivity in most sweatshop jobs, thus the standard economic model that predicts higher wages will lead to lower employment still holds.

PASSING COSTS ON TO CONSUMERS

Scholars have also claimed that increased compensation may not lead to lower employment because firms may be able to pass costs on to the consumer: "Increased labor cost may be offset by the value added to the good insofar as consumers demonstrate a preference for products produced under conditions in which the rights of workers are respected."[45] Certainly, some consumers value ethically produced items by an amount great enough to justify sweatshops paying higher total compensation. If these consumers do not decrease their quantity of purchases when prices for ethically produced goods are higher than those of other goods, a decrease in employment is not necessary. Some companies have employed this strategy successfully. But how widespread is consumer demand for ethically produced goods?

Robert Pollin and coauthors have argued that doubling the wages paid to apparel workers in Mexico would add 1.6 percent to the retail price of men's casual shirts, which is within the amount a survey suggested U.S. consumers would be willing to pay for goods produced under "good" working conditions rather than sweatshop conditions.[46] However, what U.S. consumers say they would be willing to pay is a poor substitute for actual market transactions. Ultimately, the market process must discover the demand, just as for any other product. Experimentation in production methods and marketing by different firms will be necessary. Results from surveys should be made available to companies to encourage them to consider if giving workers better wages or conditions would enhance the demand for their product. However, all consumers of sweatshop goods are unlikely to value ethically produced goods by enough to justify industry-wide higher compensation. Only through the market's competitive process can

[45] Arnold and Hartman, "Worker Rights," 29.
[46] Pollin, Burns, and Heintz, "Global Apparel Production."

the companies and producers capable of implementing this strategy be found. Ethically conscious consumers can best voice their opinions by buying ethically produced products when given the opportunity. Chapter 7 discusses voluntary ethical branding in greater detail.

COST CUTTING IN OTHER AREAS

Sweatshop critics have also claimed that increased wages, when not offset by efficiency wages or increased consumer demand, may be "readily absorbed as an operating expense" or "balanced by internal cost-cutting measures."[47] The first is highly unlikely. If a company can relocate to another country to avoid the increased wages, a profit-maximizing firm need not absorb the higher operating expense. Furthermore, wages are not a fixed cost. They are a *variable cost*, that is, one that varies with the quantity of a good produced. Sweatshop labor is often paid an hourly rate or a rate per unit of output. Economics is a science that deals with marginal adjustments. Raise the marginal variable cost of labor, and firms do not have to make an all or nothing choice of continue with the same quantity of production with a lower profit or not producing anything at all. Instead, they can vary the quantity they produce. Faced with higher marginal labor costs, firms will optimize profits by cutting back production to the point at which the new higher marginal cost equals their marginal revenue. This will decrease the quantity of labor they demand.

Arnold and Hartman posit that even if firms cannot absorb the cost of higher wages as an operating expense, they could still cut costs in other areas to compensate. They suggest decreases in the number of home-country managers or cuts in "executive perks."[48] But if these things were adversely affecting profits, wouldn't companies already be cutting costs?[49] Firms are not known to leave profits on the table intentionally. Companies will cut these costs if and when doing so is beneficial. Academics are unlikely to be more aware of a company's unnecessary costs than the actual company, which has a profit incentive

---

[47] Arnold and Hartman, "Worker Rights," 29.
[48] Arnold and Hartman, "Worker Rights," 29–30.
[49] Interestingly, chief executives and their perks fit the model of efficiency wages much more closely than assembly workers.

to find these inefficiencies. Furthermore, even in cases in which costs exist that could potentially be cut, nothing ties these cuts to increases in worker wages. A profit-maximizing firm would not increase worker wages just because it found a cost to cut elsewhere. Either it is efficient to pay workers more because of consumer demand for ethically produced goods or efficiency wages or it is not efficient. If it is not efficient (in the profit-maximizing sense) to pay workers more, finding other areas of inefficiently high costs does not make it desirable to trade one inefficiency for another from a firm's perspective. The firm would simply eliminate the existing inefficiency.

ACCEPTING A LOWER RATE OF RETURN

Scholars have suggested that the cost of increased wages could be borne by owners via a lower return on equity: "In such cases, the costs of respecting workers must be regarded as a necessary condition of doing business. The point should not be problematic for any manager who recognizes the existence of basic human dignity."[50] However, it is likely to be very problematic. A higher return on equity attracts more capital to a given industry or business. Even an executive concerned with human dignity faces this constraint. A lower return on equity will limit the number of factories that firms can open and hence will limit job creation in the impoverished countries where sweatshops exist because raising the needed capital to open new factories will be harder. Appeals to human dignity will work only to the extent that they create greater value in the minds of consumers for the products that are produced. Even owners who believe they should accept a lower return on equity to be ethical will face the financing constraints of the market and will be limited in the number of jobs they can create.

CONCLUSION: THE TEXTBOOK ECONOMICS RECLAIMED

Demand curves slope down. Anyone who has ever taken a principles-of-economics class has heard that lesson many times. Sweatshop labor is no exception. Sweatshop critic John Miller summarized the position of sweatshop defenders by writing, "Their proposition is as simple as

---

[50] Arnold and Hartman, "Worker Rights," 30.

this: 'Either you believe labor demand curves are downward sloping, or you don't.' ... Of course, not to believe that demand curves are negatively sloped would be tantamount to declaring yourself an economic illiterate."[51] Although Miller himself believes that the economic defense of sweatshops is wrong, after considering the arguments put forth by him and other scholars critical of sweatshops, we have found their arguments lacking. Their supposed exceptions to the basic economic model do nothing to overturn the economic defense of sweatshops.

Sweatshop employers will employ fewer workers if the cost of hiring them rises. Workers choose to work in sweatshops because they deem them to be their best available option. Thus, mandating higher wages will involuntarily throw some of these workers into worse alternatives. This naturally leads us to ask, "How much better are the sweatshop jobs compared to the alternatives?"

---

[51] Miller, "Why Economists Are Wrong," 107.

4

Don't Cry for Me, Kathie Lee: How Sweatshop Wages Compare to Alternatives

The national media spotlight focused on sweatshops in 1996 after Charles Kernaghan of the National Labor Committee accused Kathie Lee Gifford of exploiting children in Honduran sweatshops. He flew a fifteen-year-old worker, Wendy Diaz, to the United States to meet Kathie Lee. Kathie Lee exploded into tears and apologized on the air, promising to pay higher wages.

Should Kathie Lee have cried? Wendy reportedly earned 31 cents per hour. Assuming that Wendy worked six days per week for ten hours per day – which is not uncommon in a sweatshop – she would have earned $967.00 over the course of a year. That translates into approximately $2.75 per day to live on. But in 1996, more than 15 percent of Hondurans lived on less than $1.00 per day, and nearly 30 percent lived on less than $2.00 per day. Wendy's income is not just higher than that of people in abject poverty; it is $262.00 above the average income in Honduras that year.

Wendy Diaz's message should have been, "Don't cry for me, Kathie Lee. Cry for the Hondurans not fortunate enough to work for you." Instead, all too often, people in the United States compared 31 cents per hour to U.S. alternatives, not Honduran alternatives. But U.S. alternatives are irrelevant. No one is offering these workers green cards. The real question is how the jobs compare to other domestically available alternatives.

When economists have defended sweatshops, they have often compared a sweatshop job to a much worse alternative such as prostitution, scavenging, or agricultural work. This chapter will examine sweatshops and their available alternatives more systematically.[1]

---

[1] Benjamin Powell and David Skarbek, "Sweatshop Wages and Third World Workers: Are the Jobs Worth the Sweat?" *Journal of Labor Research* 27, No. 2 (2006), was the

THE SWEATSHOP JOBS

Sweatshops were described in the introduction to this book as places with pay well below levels in the developed world, where hours are often long and unpredictable, there is a high risk of injury on the job, and working conditions are generally unhealthy. Other characteristics might include a lack of lunch or bathroom breaks, verbal abuse, mandatory overtime, or the breaking of local labor laws. Although this general description encompasses much of what people think of when they hear of a "sweatshop," it does not get us very far in developing a specific list of sweatshops to compare to available alternatives.

No nice, neat international database of sweatshop jobs is available to download and compare to the alternatives. Monster.com does not have a "sweatshop" category either. Using the above criteria to identify sweatshops leaves us with more questions than answers. Just how low does the wage have to be for the factory to be considered a sweatshop? How many of the poor working conditions have to be present, and how bad do those conditions have to be? Should we stick only to cases in which ILO core labor standards are broken? Or only to cases in which local labor laws are broken? Ultimately, any line set would be a bit arbitrary and would open the door for accusations of defining sweatshops in such a way as to bias the result when they are compared to other alternatives.

As an alternative to creating a set definition of a sweatshop and then identifying firms that qualify, this chapter uses popular news sources to identify sweatshops. Major U.S. and international news sources were searched using Lexis Nexis. The criterion for inclusion was simple: any time a reporter or their source referred to a Third World factory as a "sweatshop," the case was included in the sample. Every effort was made to eliminate duplicate cases so that each example included in this chapter is a unique sweatshop job. In rare instances, it was evident that the workers were truly slave laborers who were forced with the threat of violence to work at the job. These examples were excluded from the sample because this book condemns slave labor and there is no reason to think that it might be superior to other available alternatives. If it

first research to systematically compare sweatshop jobs with their alternatives. This chapter follows a similar methodology, and updates their data with instances of sweatshops since 2004, when their study left off.

were, companies would not need to threaten violence to convince workers to take and keep the jobs.

This empirical method of identifying sweatshops has one main advantage: it includes every newsworthy instance of a job in the Third World that someone in the First World has thought deplorable enough to call a sweatshop. Thus, the sample is not biased to exclude either the worst of the worst or the best of the worst. However, this method does have two drawbacks. The first is that because many wages were quoted in the news sources in U.S. dollars per hour (day, so forth), it is impossible to know precisely how each wage was calculated. In some cases, the reporter may have extrapolated from a per piece rate; in other cases an hourly or weekly rate may have required an assumption about hours worked. Of course, then some exchange rate was used to turn the wage into dollars. Although this is less than ideal, there is no reason to believe that this limitation systematically biases the data in any particular direction.

The second limitation stems from how the news sources learned the wage being paid. Often reporters use anti-sweatshop activists as sources, and even quote wage rates directly from them. Even if activists do not intentionally lie, they might be biased to use the least charitable interpretation of how a given piece or hourly rate turns into overall earnings, or they might choose brand-new workers with no experience at a firm as an example rather than a more average employee. This may lead to an understatement of sweatshop earnings, and thus an understatement of how well sweatshops compare to other domestic alternatives. There is no way to correct this bias, so it should be kept in mind when evaluating comparisons later in this chapter.

From 1995 through 2010, eighty-five unique sweatshops in eighteen countries were reported in major news sources in the First World. With the exceptions of Mauritius and South Africa, all were located in Latin America or Asia. Bangladesh, China, India, and Indonesia accounted for just over 60 percent of the cases. Table 4.1 contains each individual sweatshop job. Often, the sweatshops are subcontractors selling to major multinational brands, so in many cases the articles did not identify with which multinational they were contracted, but this information is reported when available.

As is evident from the table, the wages paid in these sweatshops are deplorably low by U.S. standards. Hourly pay ranged from a low of

Table 4.1 *Sweatshop Wages Reported in the Press*

Country	Year	Company	Reported Wage	Per
Bangladesh	2010		$23.52	month
Bangladesh	2010		$30.89	month
Bangladesh	2010		$31.24	month
Bangladesh	2009		$3.50	week
Bangladesh	2009		$0.06	hour
Bangladesh	2008		$0.10	hour
Bangladesh	2008		$23.78	month
Bangladesh	2006		$13.30	month
Bangladesh	2005		$0.21	hour
Bangladesh	2004	Mary Kate & Ashley	$0.18	hour
Bangladesh	2004	H&M	$0.07	hour
Bangladesh	2004	Mary Kate & Ashley	$0.08	hour
Bangladesh	1997		$0.25	hour
Brazil	2007		$170.00	month
Brazil	2004		$65.00	month
Burma	2004	NBA	$0.14	hour
Burma	2004	NBA	$0.07	hour
Cambodia	2004		$2.00	day
China	2007	Apple, Compaq, Nokia, Sony	$50.00	month
China	2006	Apple	$50.00	month
China	2005	Disney	$0.32	hour
China	2005		$120.70	month
China	2005	Make Poverty History Campaign	$0.17	hour
China	2005		$0.69	hour
China	2004	NFL, NBA, MLB	$0.17	hour
China	2004	NBA	$0.16	hour
China	2004		$1.00	day
China	2002		$0.12	hour
China	2001		$0.20	hour
China	2001		$0.15	hour
China	1998		$0.13	hour
China	1998		$0.30	hour
China	1997	Nike	$1.75	day
China	1997		$16.00	month
China	1996		$25.00	month
Costa Rica	1998	Rawlings Baseball	$1.12	hour
Dominican Republic	2008		$7.29	day
Dominican Republic	2000		$0.69	hour

Table 4.1 (*cont.*)

Country	Year	Company	Reported Wage	Per
El Salvador	2001	Gap	$0.55	hour
El Salvador	2001	Gap	$0.60	hour
El Salvador	2001	Gap	$30.00	week
Haiti	2010		$14.39	week
Haiti	2004		$0.55	hour
Haiti	1996	Disney	$0.28	hour
Honduras	1996	Levi's and Nike	$5.40	day
Honduras	1995		$0.30	hour
Honduras	2003	P Diddy	$0.75	hour
Honduras	1996	Wal-Mart/Kathie Lee	$0.31	hour
India	2010		$0.41	hour
India	2010		$130.54	month
India	2010		$107.00	month
India	2010		$98.44	month
India	2008		$0.32	hour
India	2008		$0.40	hour
India	2008	Banana Republic	$0.30	hour
India	2007		$34.16	month
India	2007		$2.47	day
India	2007		$2.41	day
India	2007		$76.57	month
Indonesia	2004	H&M	$1.00	day
Indonesia	2004	Adidas, Jansport	$110.19	month
Indonesia	2004	Nike	$2.00	day
Indonesia	2002	Nike	$0.27	hour
Indonesia	1997	Nike	$2.46	day
Indonesia	1996	Nike	$2.28	day
Indonesia	1996		$117.00	month
Indonesia	1996	Nike	$115.00	month
Indonesia	1996	Nike	$0.14	hour
Indonesia	1996	Nike	$0.22	hour
Indonesia	1996	Nike	$0.45	hour
Laos	2010		$1.60	day
Mauritius	2007	Topshop (Designer Kate Moss)	$8.02	day
Mauritius	2007		$0.62	hour
Nicaragua	2004	Talbots, JC Penney, Eddie Bauer, Kmart	$0.50	hour
Nicaragua	2001		$135.50	week
Nicaragua	2000	Kohl's dept. stores	$3.00	day
Nicaragua	2000		$0.17	hour
Nicaragua	2000		$0.19	hour

Table 4.1 (*cont.*)

Country	Year	Company	Reported Wage	Per
Nicaragua	2000		$0.20	hour
South Africa	2010		$11.10	week
South Africa	2010		$14.39	week
Thailand	2006		$2.00	day
Vietnam	2004	NBA	$0.15	hour
Vietnam	2000	Nike	$564.00	year
Vietnam	1997	Nike	$1.60	day

6 cents per hour in Bangladesh to a high of only $1.12 per hour in Costa Rica. In general, Latin American sweatshops tended to pay more than Asian ones. Earnings were roughly two and a half times higher in Latin American sweatshops than in Asian sweatshops.

Unfortunately, when many people in the First World see these wages reported in the press, they conclude that these must be "bad" jobs. As the remainder of this chapter will demonstrate, nothing could be further from the truth. Although these wages are poor by First World standards, they are better than those for many of the jobs available in the countries where they are located.

COMPARING SWEATSHOP WAGES TO DOMESTIC ALTERNATIVES

As bad as sweatshop jobs are, of course they look good when compared to dire alternatives such as prostitution, begging, or starvation. But in most cases, people who lose their job in a sweatshop will not end up in these dire alternatives. Instead, they will end up employed in some other job in their economy, which could be in another factory or in an alternative industry, such as agriculture. Sweatshop jobs need to be compared to these common alternatives.

In countries where sweatshops tend to be located, large portions of the population work in agriculture. In Bangladesh, Cambodia, Haiti, Laos, Burma (Myanmar), and Vietnam more than half of the population is employed in agriculture. Agriculture accounts for less than 25 percent of employment in only six of the eighteen countries where

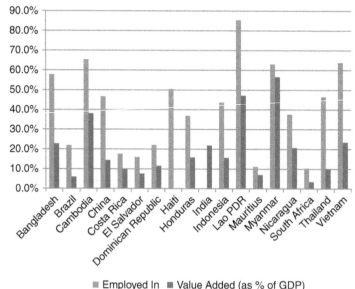

■ Employed In   ■ Value Added (as % of GDP)

Figure 4.1 Alternatives in agriculture.

sweatshops were reported (and three of these countries are anomalies that will be explained shortly). However, although large segments of the population are employed in agriculture, they fail to create a proportional share of output. Figure 4.1 illustrates the percentage of the population employed in agriculture and the percentage of total gross domestic product (GDP) that comes from the agricultural sector.

In every country where sweatshops have been reported, the share of the population working in agriculture is greater than the proportion of output the agricultural sector contributes to the economy. For example, in Bangladesh, nearly 58 percent of the population is employed in agriculture, but these people create less than 23 percent of the value of Bangladesh's economy. Overall, in sweatshop-containing countries, an average of 38 percent of people are employed in agriculture, but they create only 18 percent of the economic output. Productivity per employee in agriculture in these countries is low. As explained in Chapter 3, the upper bound of worker compensation is limited by worker productivity. When workers lose jobs in sweatshops and are reemployed in agriculture, they move into a low-productivity sector

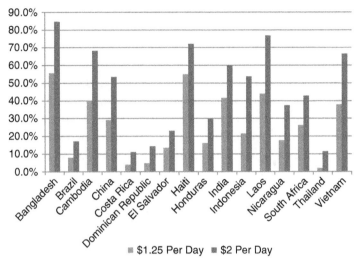

Figure 4.2 Percent of population living on less than $1.25 and
$2.00 per day (PPP).

that has a low upper bound of compensation, and can expect to earn
low wages while toiling under the sun.

Poverty abounds throughout many areas of these economies. The
World Bank tracks data on the percent of the population in countries
around the world that lives on less than $1.25 and $2.00 per day. Of
course, because $1.00 will buy more in one country than it will in
another, the World Bank adjusts the figures for purchasing power
parity (PPP) so that the $2.00 and $1.25 figures it reports represent
the same standard of living across countries. As Figure 4.2 illustrates, a
large portion of the population in sweatshop-containing countries lives
in abject poverty conditions.[2]

In every country, more than 10 percent of the population lives on
less than $2.00 per day, and in more than half of the countries, more
than 40 percent of the population does.[3] Even the $1.25 per day stand-
ard is not reached by more than 25 percent of the population in half of

---

[2] Data was unavailable for Burma and Mauritius.

[3] The table reports the average percent of the population falling in these categories for the
years that data was available from the World Bank, or the closest available years, during
the period when cases of sweatshops were reported in the news for each individual
country. In most cases these numbers were relatively stable. China and Vietnam are the
two major exceptions because of the growth that they have experienced (India grew, but

the countries. These are the relevant alternatives to which sweatshop jobs can be compared.

To make the relevant comparison, the sweatshop wages reported in Table 4.1 need to be converted to average daily income and adjusted for purchasing power parity. Working five twelve-hour days or six ten-hour days in a sweatshop is not uncommon. After all, long working hours are a defining characteristic of sweatshops. Thus, a sixty-hour, six-day work week is assumed.[4] All reported wages were converted into local currencies and then adjusted for purchasing power parity using World Bank data.[5]

Contrary to claims that sweatshop "workers are still being paid a poverty wage" by activists such as Jim Keady, the sweatshop jobs studied here compare quite favorably to the abject poverty in these countries.[6] Out of the eighty-three specific sweatshop jobs for which we could calculate earnings, seventy-seven resulted in workers earning more than $2.00 per day. Of the six exceptions, five are in Bangladesh. But in Bangladesh, nearly 85 percent of the population earns less than $2.00 per day, and in eight of the thirteen reported Bangladesh sweatshop cases, the workers earned more than $2.00 per day. Even in the five exceptions, workers earned more than the $1.25 per day standard, something that more than half of the population of the country fails to achieve. The one other instance of a sweatshop job resulting in earnings of less than $2.00 per day occurred in China in 1997. At that time, more than 65 percent of the Chinese population was living on less than $2.00 per day and more than 36 percent lived on less than $1.25, a standard that this sweatshop lifted its workers above.[7] Figure 4.3 shows the

all of the reported cases of sweatshops were within a short period of time). For instance, the percent of Chinese failing to earn $2.00 per day fell from 65 percent at the beginning of the period to 36.3 percent by the end. For Vietnam, the corresponding figures are 78.3 percent and 52.5 percent.

[4] Then annual incomes were calculated for each sweatshop job. That figure was then divided by 352 days to account for the nonworking days on which workers would have to live off their earnings.

[5] The PPP conversion factor was not yet available for 2010, so the few 2010 sweatshop cases were converted using 2009 data. Data for Burma was again unavailable.

[6] Jim Keady, "When Will Nike 'Just Do It' on the Sweatshop Issue?" *Huffington Post*, October 2, 2009.

[7] Figure 4.2 reports the average number of people in poverty over the entire period when sweatshops were reported. Because much of China's growth occurred after 1997, a much larger fraction of the population was impoverished in 1997 than is illustrated in Figure 4.2.

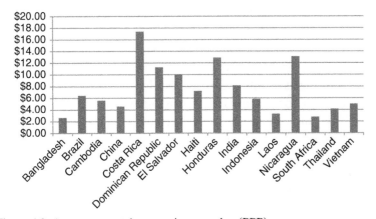

Figure 4.3 Average sweatshop earnings per day (PPP).

average amount per day that workers in each sweatshop country had to live on.

Compared to the large segments of the population in each of these countries living on less than $2.00 per day, the people working in sweatshop jobs had a superior standard of living. As Figure 4.2 illustrated, smaller fractions of the populations of Latin American countries lived on less than $2.00 per day. Note that it is in these same Latin American countries that sweatshops tend to pay wages that are many multiples greater than the $2.00 per day standard. The average sweatshop worker in Costa Rica, the Dominican Republic, El Salvador, Honduras, and Nicaragua lives on more than $10.00 per day.

Some caution is in order when making these direct comparisons. The statistics for the fraction of a population living on less than $2.00 per day account for the fact that some workers are supporting their families as well as themselves. A single mother who has one child would need to earn $4.00 per day working in a sweatshop to lift herself and her child above the $2.00 per day standard. Many sweatshop workers are young and childless, or children themselves. For these workers, the preceding comparisons of the standard of living the sweatshop job provides compared to the standard of living of other people in their country is the most accurate. In addition, many mothers working in sweatshops have husbands who earn an income as well, so much of the earnings of the mother may accurately represent her standard of living. To the extent that sweatshop earnings support the workers themselves, Figure 4.3 accurately portrays their living standards.

Although the sweatshop jobs provide a substantial improvement over the dire poverty in these countries, the bar of comparison can be raised higher. Average sweatshop earnings can be compared to the average level of income in a country rather than to poverty levels of income.

To make the comparison, all sweatshop earnings were converted into an annual income. Hourly data was converted under four different assumptions about the number of hours worked per week (forty, fifty, sixty, or seventy hours). The sixty- and seventy-hour work weeks are likely more accurate given the long hours worked in most sweatshops. Daily data were converted assuming a six-day work week, and weekly and monthly data were simply multiplied by fifty-two and twelve, respectively. Then the annual sweatshop earnings for each country were averaged.[8] Figure 4.4 shows the average sweatshop earnings in each country as a percent of GDP per capita.[9]

Although the results are less dramatic than when compared to abject poverty, sweatshop jobs still compare well with the average income in most of these countries. Working in an average sweatshop in Cambodia, Costa Rica, Haiti, Honduras, Nicaragua, and Vietnam raises a worker's income above the average for the country. In fact, in Haiti, Honduras, and Nicaragua sweatshop workers earn more than twice the national average. It is no wonder that Paul Collier endorsed a sweatshop model of development for Haiti after a disastrous hurricane struck in 2010.

In Bangladesh, El Salvador, India, and Indonesia, the average sweatshop worker earns between 80 and 100 percent of the average income, whereas in China and Laos, they earn between 50 and 60 percent of the average income. It is worth noting that the low average incomes in these countries does not reflect the median wage job, as the average income is pulled upward by the small portion of the very rich people in these

---

[8] The per capita GDP data was also averaged. For each reported sweatshop, the corresponding year's GDP per capita figure was entered into the average. Thus, the GDP per capita average is weighted to match the number of occurrences of a sweatshop in a given year. For example, if a country had four reported cases of sweatshops – one in 1998, two in 2002, and one in 2007 – the GDP would be averaged from 1998, 2002, 2002 (again), and 2007.

[9] In countries for which data was available only for daily, weekly, and monthly earnings but not hourly earnings, each of the four hourly assumptions generates the same height bar.

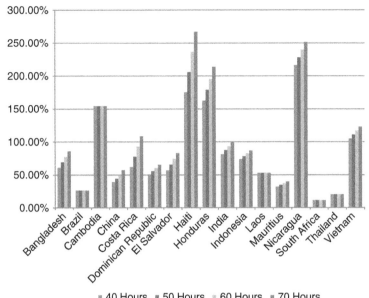

Figure 4.4 Average sweatshop earnings as a percent of average incomes.

countries. It is also important to keep in mind that just because a job falls below average does not mean it is a bad job *for the worker who chooses it*. By definition, many of the jobs in any economy will earn below the average. The key, as explained in Chapter 3, is that workers will choose the best alternative available to them. These comparisons illustrate that not only are sweatshop jobs the best available for the individual worker, but in many cases are better than alternatives available to the vast majority of the people in a country. In other cases, sweatshop jobs are far from the worst jobs in the economy, and earnings are not far below the average.

A few countries stand out as anomalies. Workers in firms accused of being sweatshops in Brazil, Mauritius, South Africa, and Thailand all, on average, earn less than 50 percent of the average income in their countries, sometimes significantly less. In each case there is a good explanation why these sweatshops do not compare as favorably as those in other countries. In Brazil, Mauritius, and Thailand, the sweatshops employed immigrants, often illegal, from even poorer countries, not native citizens. In Brazil, the sweatshop workers are Bolivians. According to the *Miami Herald*, many of sweatshop owners pay to smuggle Bolivian workers into the country illegally.[10] Threats of deportation are common, but workers continue to come. Although the $2,040.00 a sweatshop worker in Brazil earned in 2007 is small compared to Brazil's average income of $7,185.00, it exceeds the average income of Bolivia by more than $600.00.

Similarly, in Mauritius, the sweatshop workers come from Sri Lanka, India, and Bangladesh. According to the article reporting the case, the workers paid agents to obtain them the jobs, and firms paid different wages to different employees on the basis of their country of origin.[11] Although the average sweatshop wage of more than $2,200.00 does not compare favorably with Mauritius's average income of nearly $6,000.00, it is considerably above the average incomes in Bangladesh ($434.00), India ($1,096.00), and Sri Lanka ($1,617.00). The situation in Thailand is the same. *Newsweek* reports, "Thailand's surging economy has sucked in 2 million to 4 million workers from neighboring Burma, Laos and Cambodia, who gladly accept half the $4-a-day legal minimum wage for thankless factory and sweatshop jobs that many native Thais wouldn't touch."[12] The $624.00 a sweatshop worker would earn in Thailand is above Laos's average income of $589.00 and Cambodia's $518.00. Reliable income statistics are not available from Burma. This in and of itself gives an indication of how poor Burmese workers are.

China, although not an extreme outlier such as Brazil, Mauritius, and Thailand, also has lower sweatshop earnings as percent of average income than most of the other countries. Many of the Chinese sweatshop workers are Chinese, but here, too, immigration plays a role in depressing the statistics. The title of a *Los Angeles Times* article speaks for itself: "An Influx of Illegal Workers; Sound Familiar? It's Happening in China, Where the Pay Looks Good to Vietnamese."[13] The article reports that the Vietnamese workers earn more than twice as much

---

[10] Jack Chang, "Bolivians Fail to Find Better Life in Brazil; Bolivians Are Migrating to Brazil in Search of a Better Life, but Many End Up Working under Harsh Conditions and Earning Low Pay," *Miami Herald*, December 28, 2007.

[11] Jennifer Whitehead, "Topshop Faces Accusations of Using Sweatshop Labour," *Brand Republic*, August 14, 2007.

[12] Mac Margolis, "Roads to Nowhere; More and More Migrants from Poor Countries Are Heading to Other Former Backwaters for Work," *Newsweek*, September 11, 2006.

[13] David Pierson, "An Influx of Illegal Workers; Sound Familiar? It's Happening in China, Where the Pay Looks Good to Vietnamese," *Los Angeles Times*, September 19, 2010.

in Chinese sweatshops than they could at home. Not every article on Chinese sweatshops indicates whether the workers are Chinese or illegal immigrants, so precisely how much immigration causes Chinese sweatshop wages to appear less attractive than other domestic alternatives is not known. However, it certainly has some impact on making these numbers look less attractive than they otherwise would. Internal migration also plays a large role in China. China has large income inequalities between regions. Many articles report rural Chinese in poor inland provinces migrating to richer coastal provinces to work in sweatshops. Thus, using national income data overstates the alternatives available to many of the sweatshop workers.

The final anomaly was South Africa. In this case, immigration was not a factor. Rural firms refused to pay the nationally mandated minimum wage that metro firms were paying. According to the *Financial Mail*, the rural firms took advantage of "rural unemployment to pay sweatshop wages."[14] Although these rural wages do not compare favorably to the average national income, the workers here clearly believed the jobs were the best available to them in their geographic area. According to the report, "When the council attempted to exercise writs in execution against first offenders in Newcastle, desperate clothing workers threatened to assault officials and burn their vehicles rather than lose their jobs, some paying as little as R80/week."[15]

CONCLUSION

Working in a sweatshop producing clothes for Kathie Lee Gifford raised Wendy Diaz's standard of living above that of many Hondurans who earned less than $2.00 per day. In fact, Wendy earned more than the average Honduran that year. The Kathie Lee Gifford case is not an outlier; it is the norm.

Workers in firms accused of being sweatshops almost universally earn more than $2.00 per day. However, large portions of the population in each of these countries live on less than $2.00 per day. Working in a sweatshop in three of these countries results in workers earning more

---

[14] Claire Bisseker, "Clothing Industry. Policy Doesn't Fit Practice," *Financial Mail* (South Africa), September 10, 2010.

[15] Bisseker, "Clothing Industry."

than twice the average national income, and in another three countries it lifts workers above the average. In another four countries, sweatshop workers earn 80 percent or more of the average. In the exceptions in which earnings are considerably below average, the workers appear to be immigrants who are earning more than the average income in their home countries. In short, these sweatshop jobs pay wages that are not just superior to earnings from begging or prostitution. They pay better than many of the other opportunities available to sweatshop workers and make them better off than many of their fellow countrymen. If the wages are superior to other opportunities, then activists might naturally ask if they should turn their attention to improving other working conditions instead. That is what we consider next.

5

Health, Safety, and Working Conditions Laws

Sweatshop critics are often more upset about the conditions under which the workers toil than about the wages the workers are paid. Sometimes sweatshop critics even admit that the wages are better than alternative available employment, and make the working conditions their sole focus.[1]

A November 2012 factory fire in Bangladesh sparked worldwide outrage over safety conditions. The Tarzeen factory, which made cloths for Wal-Mart and Disney, was denied a renewal of its fire safety certificate the previous June because of safety violations, but it continued operating without the certificate. Then tragedy struck, when a fire ripped through the eight-story building, killing 112 garment workers who were trapped inside. Subsequent investigations found that a quarter of the factories operating in the industrial zone where Tarzeen was located lacked fire safety certificates. The executive director of the Bangladesh Center for Worker Solidarity, Kalpona Aktar, spoke what many felt when she said, "These factories should be shut down."[2] But, as tragic as this fire was, is she right? Would workers be better off if factories that do not comply with safety standards are prohibited?

Critics are correct that working conditions in sweatshops are often horrid compared to those in the United States. Fires such as the one

[1] For instance, Bama Athreya, from the International Labor Rights Fund, admitted that wages in sweatshops were typically higher than in domestic industry, but argued that the working conditions need to be addressed in a public debate with me at Grand Valley State December 1, 2008.

[2] Associated Press, "Factory in Bangladesh Lost Fire Clearance before Blaze," *New York Times*, December 7, 2012. Retrieved from http://www.nytimes.com/2012/12/08/world/asia/bangladesh-factory-where-dozens-died-was-illegal.html?_r=0.

at Tarzeen are an extreme case, but other conditions are also poor. Workers can be at risk of on-the-job injuries from dangerous machines. Sometimes air quality is poor and could lead to long-term health problems. The ILO estimates that 6,300 people die every day, more than 2.3 million per year, as a result of occupational accidents or work-related diseases.[3] Sometimes it is the other general working conditions that are bad. Factories may be crowded, dirty, and hot. Hours can be long, breaks short or nonexistent, overtime mandatory and unpredictable. Vacations, paid or otherwise, might not be allowed. Six-day work weeks are common, and some people work seven. Often, legally mandated benefits are not provided.

As bad as working conditions are in sweatshops, much like wages, the conditions in alternative employment are often worse. For example, although conditions in Cambodian sweatshops can be poor, the alternative of scavenging in the Phnom Penh garbage dump is much worse. *New York Times* columnist Nicolas Kristof reports that the dump is a "Dante-like vision of hell. It's a mountain of festering refuse, a half hour hike across, emitting clouds of smoke from subterranean fires."[4] Yet small, barefoot children scavenge for old plastic cups that they can sell for 5 cents a pound. Kristof interviewed nineteen-year-old Pim Srey Rath, who was scavenging in the dump. She said, "I'd loved to get a job in a factory. At least that work is in the shade. Here is where it is hot." Thirteen-year-old scavenger Neuo Chanthou, whose sister lost part of her hand when a garbage truck ran over her, sums up the situation concisely by saying, "It's dirty, hot, and smelly here. A factory is better."

Activists again have to be careful not to advocate for changes that may eliminate lousy sweatshop working conditions and throw workers into even worse conditions elsewhere. Dan Viederman, the CEO of Verité, an NGO "committed to ensuring that people in factories and farms work under safe, fair, and legal conditions," makes an argument that is typical of anti-sweatshop activists. In a recent column he wrote, "I'm always amazed to come across opinion pieces that claim sweatshops are good for workers."[5] Why? Because sweatshop defenders

---

[3] ILO, "Safety and Health at Work," retrieved from http://www.ilo.org/global/topics/safety-and-health-at-work/lang--en/index.htm.

[4] Nicolas Kristof, "Where Sweatshops Are a Dream," *New York Times*, January 14, 2009.

[5] Dan Viederman, "Any Job Is a Good Job? Think Again," *Huffington Post*, February 18, 2011.

"don't mention whether or not there are minimum standards that the job should meet. This is a pretty massive oversight."[6] Viederman claims to solve the problem for us: "Luckily for the pro-sweatshop crowd, there are already widely accepted ways of deciding whether a job is good enough, and whether kids are acceptable employees, so they won't have to think too hard about these complicated problems. These are the international standards of the International Labor Organization."[7] Rather than accept Viederman's suggestion, I invite you to think hard about these complicated problems as the remainder of this chapter examines whether mandating ILO working-condition regulations would improve the lives of sweatshop workers or not.

Chapters 3 and 4 focused mostly on how wages were determined and how sweatshop wages compared to alternative employment. When workers choose to work for a firm they obviously also take working conditions into account. Employees care about how much they are paid, but also whether their job is safe and the conditions pleasant. Thus, a dangerous job, all else equal, demands a higher wage to attract workers.[8]

Consider dangerous professions in the United States. Jobs in fishing, mining, and truck driving all pay well considering the typical level of education of the workers. But all are relatively dangerous professions compared to U.S. alternatives.[9] As a result, they must pay more to attract enough workers. However, the level of safety in these jobs is much higher in the United States than it is in other countries. In mining, for instance, the death rate per ton of coal extracted is 100 times lower in the United States than it is in China.[10] If the U.S. conditions were as unsafe as the Chinese conditions, wages would need to go even higher to attract workers. To put it differently, relatively wealthy workers in the United States "buy" better safety conditions by sacrificing wages. Relatively poorer Chinese workers cannot afford that level of safety.

---

[6] Ibid.

[7] Ibid.

[8] Michael Moore and Kip Viscusi, *Compensation Mechanisms for Job Risks* (Princeton: Princeton University Press, 1990).

[9] See Tom Van Riper, "America's Most Dangerous Jobs," *Forbes*, August 13, 2007, retrieved from http://www.forbes.com/2007/08/13/dangerous-jobs-fishing-lead-careers-cx_tvr_0813danger.html, for a list of the most dangerous professions in the United States.

[10] Tyler Cowen and Alex Tabbarrok, *The New Principles* (New York: Worth, 2009).

Some critics of sweatshops want to separate the analysis of wages from the analysis of working conditions.[11] Some will admit that mandating higher wages may result in unemployment, but want to maintain that health and safety can be improved without unemploying workers. This is not true; the two are jointly determined.

Compensation can be paid directly as wages or indirectly as benefits, which may include health, safety, comfort, longer breaks, and fewer working hours. Some indirect payments can raise worker productivity. Obviously, employing healthy workers who can perform their jobs positively impacts profits. Some firms may thus choose to provide subsidized lunches, health care, and on-the-job safety that increases worker productivity. In fact, it is in firms' best interests to contribute this form of indirect compensation. However, if these benefits cost more than the revenue gain from increased productivity, then firms do not increase their profits because of them. In these cases, the firm regards such benefits as costs that come off their bottom line, just like wages. A profit-maximizing firm is indifferent to compensating workers with pay or health, safety, leisure, and comfort benefits of the same cost when productivity is unaffected. The firm simply cares about the overall cost of the total compensation package.

Workers, on the other hand, do care about the mix of compensation they receive. When overall compensation goes up, workers are more likely to desire more nonmonetary benefits. Comfort and safety are what economists call "normal goods" for most people. Workers demand more of these goods as their income increases. Unfortunately, many workers have low productivity, so their overall compensation level is low. As such, they demand most of their compensation in wages and little in health or safety improvements. This is why U.S. miners "buy" more safety than Chinese miners.

This presents a problem for those who wish to separate safety and working conditions from pay. Both are limited by the same factor – the worker's marginal revenue product. Firms are indifferent about whether to pay monetary wages or in-kind benefits after adjusting for those benefits that improve productivity. Workers do care about the

---

[11] Denis Arnold and Laura Hartman, "Worker Rights and Low Wage Industrialization: How to Avoid Sweatshops," *Human Rights Quarterly* 28, No. 3 (August 2006): 576–700, is an example.

mix. As such, firms' profit incentive causes them to provide the mix of benefits and wages that their average worker desires to attract the best employees possible. If employers offer a mix of compensation and working conditions that does not match employee preferences, then firms are paying more for the compensation than the value the employee attaches to the overall compensation. A profit-maximizing firm can adjust the mix and lower its cost while still giving employees the same level of satisfaction. This means that the mix of compensation is really driven by employee preferences (limited by their overall productivity), not by the preferences of multinational corporations or their subcontractors.

Scholars have found plenty of empirical evidence that supports this economic theory. In a recent paper, economists Pavel Yakovlev and Russell Sobel studied injury rates in 353 industries in the United States from 1977 to 1989. Because firms face higher wages and injury-related costs when safety is low, it "means that labor is relatively more costly than capital in these industries once the cost of injuries is factored in. This gives firms an incentive to find and adopt new capital and technologies that reduce worker exposure to danger and lead to lower injury rates over time."[12] Empirically, this is just what they find. Industries that had higher injury rates tended to employ more capital relative to labor over time, and injuries went down as a result because fewer workers were exposed to risks and those who remained exposed faced lower levels of risk.

Economist Price Fishback also finds that compensating differentials played a role in worker pay when regulations were few and sweatshops were more prevalent in the United States.[13] He surveyed the literature on turn-of-the-century labor markets. At the time, common law entitled worker's families to compensation if they died on the job. Most families received that compensation without going to court, and the death benefit averaged about a half-year's income.[14] To supplement

---

[12] Pavel Yakovlev and Russell S. Sobel, "Occupational Safety and Profit Maximization: Friends or Foes?" *Journal of Socio-Economics* 39, No. 3 (June 2010), 435.

[13] Price Fishback, "Operations of 'Unfettered' Labor Markets: Exit and Voice in American Labor Markets at the Turn of the Century," *Journal of Economic Literature* 36, No. 2 (June 1998), 722–765.

[14] Fishback, " 'Unfettered' Labor Markets," 735.

the relatively low post-fatality benefit, workers in jobs with a higher risk of death were paid higher wages. Depending on the industry, the higher wages paid to workers implied that they valued their lives between \$32,000 and \$1.3 million (in 2010 dollars).[15] Furthermore, Fishback finds that, just as theory predicts, when "workers' compensation laws raised post-accident benefits, wages adjusted downward."[16]

What about sexual harassment in sweatshops? Numerous anti-sweatshop groups claim that female workers face sexual harassment ranging from verbal harassment to demands of sexual favors. For example, Bangalore ActionAid worker Malagi Christopher has heard terrible stories of harassment.[17] The *Daily Mail* reports that he has heard about a supervisor asking a woman for a condom and to sleep with him. "Another asked a girl, when she went to the toilet, if he could join her. Other women have been shown obscene photographs. They are often too scared to refuse the men's demands."[18] Similarly, Claudia Molina, a young Honduran worker, reported that her supervisors harassed the workers. "Sometimes they touch our breasts or buttocks, especially late at night, when we are sleepy."[19]

If the risk of sexual harassment is part of the working conditions at a factory, then firms have to offer higher wages to attract workers. This is precisely what Professor Joni Hersch found when studying U.S. labor markets. She examines sexual harassment claims and wages by industry and finds that women were paid higher wages in industries in which they were at a greater risk of sexual harassment. She concludes that workers receive a wage premium for exposure to the risk of sexual harassment "in much the same way that workers receive a wage premium for the

---

[15] Ibid. These dollar amounts are not the actual extra wages employees received. They instead take into account the probability of a fatality and the extra wages received to see what price the workers themselves implicitly put on their lives when they agreed to the job with a risk of death.

[16] Fishback, "'Unfettered Labor Markets," 735–738.

[17] ActionAid is an antipoverty organization with a variety of campaigns. Although far from their only focus, they are often critical of sweatshops.

[18] Natalie Clarke, "The True Price of the £6 Dress," *The Daily Mail*, September 13, 2007, retrieved from http://www.dailymail.co.uk/femail/article-481538/The-true-price-6-dress.html.

[19] Anne-Marie O'Connor, "The Plight of Women Around the World; Central America; Labor: Sweatshops Meet U.S. Consumer Demand," *The Atlanta Journal Constitution*, September 3, 1995.

risk of fatality or injury."[20] In short, the analysis of sexual harassment on the job is much the same as the analysis of other working conditions. Laws that effectively eliminate sexual harassment would lower wages. If employees desired this, then market forces would remix the compensation package to minimize harassment and lower wages. Claudia Molina, for example, earns $30 per week, which does not sound like a lot but amounts to an annual income of more than double the Honduran average. Some amount of that wage premium is likely a compensating differential for a greater risk of harassment.

Activists naïvely assume that demanding better working conditions will improve the lives of workers. Unfortunately, they are wrong. Improving working conditions raises firms' costs of hiring labor. A firm can respond to demands for improved working conditions in one of three ways. First, just as when higher wages are mandated, the firm can cut back on the number of workers it employs, which throws some workers into worse alternatives. Second, depending on the particular demands, the firm may improve some working conditions while making other conditions worse. For example, when confronted with demands for increased safety, the firm may compensate by requiring longer hours. Third, when working conditions improve, the firm can lower the wage necessary to attract employees.[21] The first of these responses is obviously bad for workers, but the second two are, as well, because the mix of compensation is largely driven by employee preferences. Reshuffling the mix makes workers worse off. Calls from First World activists to improve working conditions are really attempts to impose the preferences of First World activists at the expense of the preferences of the very workers they are supposedly trying to help. This is precisely what I find when my coauthor, economist J. R. Clark, and I interview sweatshop workers in Guatemala.[22]

---

[20] Joni Hersch, "Compensating Differentials for Sexual Harassment," *American Economic Review Papers and Proceedings* (May 2011), retrieved from http://papers.ssrn.com/sol3/papers.cfm?abstract_id=1743691.

[21] For one example, see R. Stern and K. Terrell, who find that raising the cost of labor through more stringent standards, particularly in developing countries where productivity is very low, leads to less employment, production, and income. "Labor Standards and the World Trade Organization," Discussion Paper No. 499 (paper presented at RSIE, University of Michigan, Ann Arbor, 2003).

[22] J. R. Clark and Benjamin Powell, "Sweatshop Working Conditions and Employee Welfare: Say It Ain't Sew," *Comparative Economics Studies* 55: 343–357 (2013).

A SURVEY OF GUATEMALAN SWEATSHOPS

The NLC investigates and exposes human and labor rights abuses committed by U.S. companies producing goods in poorer countries. It has issued hundreds of reports alleging abusive sweatshop activities in dozens of countries. The NLC identified four Guatemalan firms as sweatshops between 2006 and 2009.[23] Two of the factories, Dong Bang and Fribo, closed before we could survey workers. In 2010, we surveyed a sample of workers from the remaining two factories, Sam Bridge S. A. and Nicotex.

Sam Bridge employs more than 1,000 workers and exports clothing to the United States with Briggs New York, Koret, J. M. Collection, and Pantalogy labels, and produces uniforms for United Airlines. Sam Bridge was founded in 1993 and is located a short distance outside of Guatemala City on the Pan-American Highway.[24] Nicotex employed approximately 320 workers. About 80 percent of their production was for Briggs New York and the remaining 20 percent for Lane Bryant. It was opened in 2007 in Mixco, a suburb of Guatemala City. Nicotex recently closed.

The NLC's complaints about Sam Bridge include inadequate wages, long work hours, unpredictable overtime, penalties for workers who refuse overtime, arbitrary production goals, verbal abuse of workers, limiting water and bathroom breaks, inadequate ventilation, inadequate lunch facilities, inadequate medical care, and not paying severance to fired workers. The NLC succinctly summarized their view, writing, "Sam Bridge is definitely a sweatshop."[25] NLC released a report in February 2009 alleging that Nicotex was a harmful sweatshop. The list of complaints was similar: long and unpredictable hours, verbal abuse, inadequate wages, not paying bonus wages on time, not enrolling and paying for mandatory health care for all workers, and not giving mandated paid vacations. The NLC summarized their view,

---

[23] A fifth firm, Legumex, was also identified by the NLC. We did not include Legumex in our study because it is an agro-industrial plant rather than an apparel producer.

[24] It was originally named Sam Lucas, and again recently changed its name to SAM SOL, but ownership has remained the same.

[25] Institute for Global Labour and Human Rights, "Alert – Violation of CAFTA at Sam Bridge SA Guatemala," October 21, 2007, retrieved from http://www.nlcnet.org/alerts?id=0072.

writing that there are "illegal sweatshop conditions at the Nicotex factory."[26]

In May 2010, we surveyed a sample of thirty-five workers at each factory.[27] The NLC reports had complained that prior corporate audits were laughable: "Management chooses the workers who will speak with corporate auditors, and for this they pick the newest, youngest and most timid workers who do not know much about the factory and who are most frightened about being fired. This guarantees a short but shallow interview."[28] To avoid this problem, we did not obtain permission from either company to survey their workers. We hired a local firm, Aragón & Asociados, to randomly survey a subset of workers off of company property.[29] The surveys were conducted before the factory opened, when workers left for lunch, and when they left the factory to go home. Complete anonymity was guaranteed to each worker who completed a survey. Our method allowed us to obtain more honest responses than we would have obtained had we gained approval from the companies. It also limited our sample to thirty-five workers at each firm because of the amount of time we felt we could survey workers without drawing undue attention. We have no reason to believe that the subset of workers we interviewed is not representative of a larger population of workers.

The average worker we surveyed was thirty years old; the youngest was twenty and the oldest fifty-four years old. Slightly more than half (52.9%) of our sample were males, and the average worker had worked for their company for 3.8 years, with the newest employee only having been on the job for two months and the most senior had been there sixteen years. More than 61 percent of the people surveyed worked on the production line as apparel machine operators. An additional 8.5 percent each worked in product inspection, packing, or in a

---

[26] See Institute for Global Labour and Human Rights, "Women Exploiting Women," February 25, 2009, retrieved from http://www.nlcnet.org/reports?id=0535, for their original report.

[27] Surveys were completed over a period of three days from May 19 to May 22.

[28] Institute for Global Labour and Human Rights, "Women Exploiting Women."

[29] Aragón y Associates is headquartered in Guatemala City. Founded in 1972, they have conducted more than 5,000 research studies that have analyzed or gathered the opinions of more than 2.5 million people across Central America, the Caribbean, and South America.

supervisory role.[30] Another 7 percent worked in pressing, and 6 percent worked in some other capacity. These numbers were fairly consistent across both Sam Bridge and Nicotex.[31]

The NLC complained that Sam Bridge employees had to work long hours – often fifty-five to sixty hours in a week, which includes mandatory overtime. The workers we surveyed estimated they worked fifty-two hours a week. Only 12.5 percent of workers desired to work longer hours. More importantly, 97 percent of workers said they would not be willing to earn less in order to have fewer hours. The hours may be long, but the workers are poor and desire the hours to help feed and clothe their families.

The NLC complained that Sam Bridge managers would curse at and humiliate the workers. The NLC reports that the supervisors taunt the workers, shouting, "Do you have garbage for brains?" "Why can't you reach the goal. . . . You're all like shit, like piss water," and "It's easier to work with animals than you. You're good for nothing." However, when asked, "How would you rate how fairly the managers treat you?" all of the employees we surveyed reported "fairly" or "very fairly."

The NLC reported that managers told Sam Bridge employees that they only needed to use a bathroom once per ten-hour shift, but 91 percent of the workers surveyed reported they could go to the bathroom any time they wanted, and 6 percent said they could go up to four times per day. Only 3 percent of workers reported being limited to two bathroom breaks.

Other complaints by the NLC include a lack of fans, an inadequate medical clinic, and lack of adequate space for employees to have lunch. But all of the employees we surveyed reported that they were satisfied with their job. Most tellingly, all workers surveyed reported that they were unwilling to earn less to have more pleasant working conditions, and 97 percent were unwilling to earn less for safer working conditions.

The NLC complained that Nicotex had long mandatory overtime hours, failed to register all of its workers for mandatory health care through the Guatemalan Institute of Social Security, and alleged that

---

[30] Excluding the six employees who worked in some form of supervisory role doesn't significantly change any of our results.

[31] The exceptions were that all of our supervisory workers and most packers worked for Sam Bridge; most inspectors and pressers worked for Nicotex.

Nicotex was cheating workers out of their paid vacation. In addition to the legal forty-four-hour work week, "overtime work is common, obligatory and excessive, which is a violation of Guatemalan law. It is common for the women to be forced to work 20 to 25 hours of overtime a week."[32] Furthermore, "the workers are never notified of overtime in advance. Rather, management decides, often just 30 minutes before the shift's end, instructing the workers that they must stay."[33] Our survey revealed that Nicotex workers were averaging just more than fifty-nine hours a week. Importantly, nearly 83 percent of workers surveyed said they would not be willing to reduce the number of hours worked if it resulted in lower pay. In fact, 20 percent said they would like to work more hours. We also asked workers if they would be willing to accept lower pay if their employer made their hours more predictable. Nearly 86 percent said they would not.

Guatemalan law requires all employers to enroll their workers in the Guatemalan Institute of Social Security, which provides health and pension benefits. When workers are enrolled, 4.83 percent is deducted from their wages, and the employer contributes an additional 10.67 percent of their wages. When workers' payments are up to date, they have access to special hospitals and clinics. The NLC claims that Nicotex enrolled only 20 percent of its workers at any one time in order to avoid making larger contributions. As a result, workers could not depend on being in the enrolled minority and often would not have access to health care. We asked workers if they would be willing to accept lower pay in order to have health insurance; only 20 percent were.

Guatemalan law requires every worker to be guaranteed fifteen days paid vacation after they have worked for a firm for one year. The NLC alleged that "no worker at Nicotex has had a single day's paid vacation since the factory opened in November of 2007."[34] When asked to honor legally mandated vacation time, supervisors reportedly responded, "Forget it. Nicotex never rests. If you feel tired, then resign and go to your home. There you can sleep. The gates are wide and open. If you go, we will replace you in five minutes."[35] We asked workers if they would

[32] Institute for Global Labour and Human Rights, "Women Exploiting Women."
[33] Ibid.
[34] Ibid.
[35] Ibid.

Table 5.1 *Desirability of the Mix of Compensation*

	Nicotex		Sam Bridge		Total	
	Yes	No	Yes	No	**Yes**	**No**
Are you willing to work for lower pay if your employer:						
Reduced the number of hours you have to work?	17.1%	82.9%	2.9%	97.1%	**10.0%**	**90.0%**
Made your hours more predictable?	14.3%	85.7%	2.9%	97.1%	**8.6%**	**91.4%**
Gave you more bathroom breaks?	2.9%	97.1%	2.9%	97.1%	**2.9%**	**97.1%**
Gave you longer lunch breaks?	5.7%	94.3%	2.9%	97.1%	**4.3%**	**95.7%**
Made your working conditions more pleasant?	17.1%	82.9%	0.0%	100.0%	**8.6%**	**91.4%**
Made your working conditions safer?	5.7%	94.3%	2.9%	97.1%	**4.3%**	**95.7%**
Provided health insurance?	20.0%	80.0%	8.6%	91.4%	**14.3%**	**85.7%**
Gave you paid vacation?	31.4%	68.6%	5.7%	94.3%	**18.6%**	**81.4%**
Treated you more fairly?	20.0%	80.0%	0.0%	100.0%	**10.0%**	**90.0%**
Reduced the risk of sexual harassment?	0.0%	100.0%	0.0%	100.0%	**0.0%**	**100.0%**

be willing to earn less to have paid vacation. Nearly 69 percent of workers were unwilling to give up any pay for vacation.

Employees at both firms were asked if they would be willing to accept lower wages to improve any of ten working conditions. Some of these questions addressed specific NLC complaints at one firm or the other and some were more general. Table 5.1 summarizes their answers.

On eight of the ten questions, when both firms are averaged together, more than 90 percent of the workers answered "No." Paid vacation was the most popular improvement, but even here more than 81 percent of the workers answered that they would not sacrifice any wages for vacation. Nearly 65 percent of workers surveyed answered that they were unwilling to give up any wages for improved conditions across the board for all ten questions.

The complaints against Nicotex were released in February 2009. In August 2009, Nicotex signed an agreement with the Guatemalan Center for Studies and Support for Local Development (who had coauthored the complaint with the NLC) to improve conditions.[36] We asked workers to answer our survey based on how conditions were before the agreement was reached in our earlier questions. Next, we asked questions about how things have changed since the agreement.

According to the NLC, the agreement ensures that "the workers have won the right to healthcare. Significant health and safety improvements have been implemented. All overtime will be voluntary. Vacation time and pay will be honored. And workers are guaranteed their right to defend their legal, women's and labor rights."[37] Other provisions include greater access to water and bathroom breaks and less verbal abuse from supervisors.

We find evidence that Nicotex compensated for the demanded improvements along the margins that economic theory predicts. Twenty-six percent of workers saw their hours reduced, but before the reforms 83 percent of workers said they would be unwilling to work fewer hours if it meant earning less. We also asked workers if their pay had been reduced, and 14 percent reported it had. Nicotex also dealt with the higher cost of labor by employing fewer workers. Eighty-three percent of workers reported that fewer people worked for Nicotex in May 2010 than had before the agreement with the NLC.

When asked a general question, "Have your working conditions improved [since the agreement]?" only 31 percent answered yes; 69 percent said they had not. It is not clear whether Nicotex simply did not implement the agreed-on changes or whether it had and workers viewed the change as net lack of improvement because Nicotex compensated on other margins. However, we also asked employees, "Overall, how do you feel about your conditions [since the agreement]?" Fewer than 3 percent answered "much more satisfied," and only 17 percent answered "more satisfied." The most frequent response, given by 49 percent of the workers, was "the same." However, 31 percent of workers reported that they were "less satisfied" with their overall conditions since the agreement. This is some indication that Nicotex did implement reforms but that the

---

[36] The agreement can be found here: Institute for Global Labour and Human Rights, "Major Worker Rights Victory in Guatemala," October 13, 2009, retrieved from http://www.nlcnet.org/alerts?id=0022.

[37] Ibid.

reforms satisfied the preferences of the NLC at the expense of the preferences of the Nicotex employees.

In a follow-up visit in April 2011, we learned that Nicotex had closed in the year since our survey. Whether the closure was related to increased costs resulting from the NLC agreement or other economic forces is not possible to determine.

On net, these two surveys support the theory articulated earlier in the chapter. Working conditions may be poor by U.S. standards, but the mix roughly reflects employee preferences given their overall low level of productivity.[38] I followed up these surveys by personally visiting Sam Bridge and meeting with the owner. His statements revealed that, as theory predicts, he was indifferent to the mix of compensation he had to pay workers, but only cared about his absolute cost.[39]

Both of these cases, but Nicotex in particular, highlight a problem that occurs when worker preferences conflict with local labor laws. Should firms respect the laws or deliberately break them?

BREAKING LOCAL LABOR LAWS

Thus far, I have argued that minimum wage laws or health and safety requirements will increase the cost of labor and lead to employment of fewer sweatshop workers. But if new labor regulations are bad because they lead to unemployment, shouldn't the enforcement of existing labor regulations be bad for precisely the same reason? Other defenders of sweatshops such as Gordon Sollars and Fred Englander, who grant that

---

[38] A survey of sweatshop workers in El Salvador similarly found that workers had generally improved their working conditions (as well as their wages) compared to their prior employment. David Skarbek et al., "Sweatshops, Opportunity Costs, and Non-Monetary Compensation: Evidence from El Salvador," *American Journal of Economics and Sociology*, 71(3): 539–561 (2012).

[39] I followed up these surveys by visiting Sam Bridge and meeting with the owner/director, MyungChul Kim, April 27, 2011. I asked him if he would be willing to give paid vacation if the workers were willing to accept less in wages. He replied, "People need money, not vacations. Guatemala is very poor." When asked about shortening the hours his employees worked, he responded that the workers desired the hours but that he would like to avoid paying overtime because it costs him more money, but he has to use overtime because of the late-penalty clauses attached to U.S. orders. When asked directly if he cared whether he paid a worker the equivalent of $4.00 an hour in wages or $3.00 in wages and $1.00 in other benefits, not surprisingly, he answered that it did not matter to him.

managers of companies have moral obligations not to tolerate or encourage violations of the law, thus seem to hold an inconsistent position.[40] A more consistent view, according to Arnold and Bowie, "would seem to be that MNE [Multinational Enterprise] managers have duties to ignore local labor laws, ignore working conditions, and pay the lowest possible wages, so long as none of these practices deterred employees from working in MNE factories."[41]

In a more recent essay, Arnold writes that although defenders of sweatshops must "either deny or tacitly approve the widespread violation of labor laws that take place in global sweatshops," it is nevertheless "difficult to justify widespread violations of the law."[42] This argument is best conceived as a reductio ad absurdum. Because the pro-sweatshop argument, if followed to its logical conclusion, entails that managers have a duty to ignore local labor laws, and so forth, and because managers clearly do not have these duties, the pro-sweatshop argument clearly must be unsound. This challenge is an important one. If the violation of labor laws is required by the pro-sweatshop argument and is unjust, then the pro-sweatshop argument will need to be modified or abandoned. If, on the other hand, the violation of labor laws is justifiable, then it is incumbent upon defenders of sweatshops to provide an argument for this claim.

Arnold is correct to claim that the same logic that underlies the opposition to the increased legal regulation of sweatshops also counts against the enforcement of certain existing regulations by the state as well as the compliance with certain existing regulations by sweatshops. The essence of the response is that the violation of labor laws by sweatshops is indeed sometimes justifiable. For example, a minimum wage set above worker productivity would clearly harm local laborers. In countries where labor's marginal revenue product is $2.00 per hour, and $3.00 per hour is the minimum wage, respecting local labor laws

---

[40] Actually, what G. Sollars and F. Englander actually say is that "MNEs or their managers have duties not to tolerate or encourage violations of *the rule of law*" (emphasis added), in "Sweatshops: Kant and Consequences," *Business Ethics Quarterly* 17, No. 1 (2007), 115. Arnold and Bowie assume that violations of the law are tantamount to violations of the rule of law. I will allow this assumption for the sake of the present exposition but will return to criticize it later.

[41] Sollars and Englander, "Kant and Consequences," 139.

[42] Denis Arnold, "Working Conditions: Safety and Sweatshops," in *The Oxford Handbook of Business Ethics*, eds. George Brenkert and Tom Beauchamp (New York: Oxford University Press, 2010, 638).

will leave workers unemployed or push them into informal sector jobs. No one should recommend compliance with this local labor law if worker welfare is their goal.

Of course, this does not mean that all violations of labor laws by sweatshops are permissible. Some labor laws prohibit actions that defenders of sweatshops can, consistent with their pro-sweatshop position, hold to be indefensible on moral and economic grounds. The opposition to forced labor, for instance, is not only consistent with the logic of the pro-sweatshop position, but arguably a presupposition of it. Sweatshops therefore should comply with laws that prohibit forced labor, not because such laws make forced labor illegal, but because forced labor would be immoral and inefficient regardless of its legal status. Furthermore, it is sometimes in workers' interest for firms to comply with even bad laws when the costs of noncompliance would be excessively high. Suppose, for instance, that a country has a law stipulating a minimum wage above the market-clearing wage for a certain form of unskilled labor. The standard position of defenders of sweatshops is that such a law is a bad law insofar as it tends to lead to greater unemployment among unskilled laborers. Nevertheless, if the law is enforced, perhaps by the imposition of monetary fines on noncompliant firms, a firm might have decisive moral and economic reason to comply with it because doing so might be necessary to remain in business and continue employing any labor at all. In complying with the minimum wage law, the firm may be forced to employ less than the optimal number of workers, but it would be even further from the optimal number if it was forcibly shut down by government enforcement efforts.

Defenders of sweatshops are therefore not logically committed to approving of all labor law violations, but the logic of our position does push toward the approval of some such violations. What makes the difference? Some scholars have suggested that the defense of sweatshops, and the case for violation of labor regulations, is based solely on the value of "economic efficiency."[43] But this is a mistake. No serious

---

[43] See, for instance, Denis Arnold and Norman Bowie, "Sweatshops and Respect for Persons," *Business Ethics Quarterly* 13, No. 2 (April 2003), 228 ("The intentional violation of the legal rights of workers in the interest of economic efficiency is fundamentally incompatible with the duty of MNEs to respect workers."); Denis Arnold and Laura Hartman, "Beyond Sweatshops: Positive Deviancy and Global Labour Practices," *Business Ethics: A European Review* 14, No. 3 (July 2005), 212 (on the

academic defense of sweatshops has ever been based primarily on the idea of economic efficiency, and thus to the extent that the arguments given by such persons logically commit them to approving of the violation of labor regulations, that approval must be based on some other value.[44]

That value is the very same one endorsed by critics of sweatshops: the welfare of citizens in the Third World.[45] Defenders of sweatshops should endorse the violation of labor laws when that violation would benefit citizens of the Third World.[46] But if defenders of sweatshops base their position on the same basic value as that embraced by opponents of sweatshops, what explains the difference in their conclusions?

Part of the difference stems from empirical disagreements. I believe that there are some cases in which disregarding labor regulations would be better for workers than adhering to them. If, for instance, workers

need to move the sweatshop debate "beyond the entrenched, polarized, political narrative of economic efficiency versus increased regulatory protection for workers' rights"); Denis Arnold and Laura Hartman, "Worker Rights and Low Wage Industrialization: How to Avoid Sweatshops," *Human Rights Quarterly* 28, No. 3 (August 2006), 690 ("Those who are genuinely interested in the welfare of the citizens of developing nations ought to demand that MNCs and their contractors respect local labor laws, rather than excusing those MNCs that violate local laws in the name of economic efficiency").

[44] Arnold et al. are never entirely clear regarding what they mean by the term "economic efficiency." One standard understanding of the term, however, holds that an arrangement is economically efficient if the total benefits it generates could not be produced at a lower cost. To say that an arrangement is economically efficient, on this understanding, is to make a claim about aggregate costs and benefits, and therefore requires some method of measuring and summing costs and benefits interpersonally. Furthermore, to say that the violation of labor laws is justified on grounds of economic efficiency would be to say that the aggregate benefits of such violations outweigh the aggregate costs. Such a claim, it is worth noting, is compatible with the violation of harming workers and other citizens of developing countries as a class as long as the gains to, say, the company or its consumers are large enough. In contrast, every serious academic defense of sweatshops has been based not on the generalized aggregate benefits that sweatshops produce, but on the benefits that they produce specifically for workers and citizens of the developing world. This is true of Ian Maitland, Matt Zwolinski, Gordon Sollars, Fred Englandern, and myself.

[45] Arnold and Hartman, "Worker Rights," 690.

[46] The choice of "citizens" rather than "workers" is deliberate. Adhering to or violating labor regulations obviously affects the workers who are subject to those regulations. But to the extent that such regulations affect the cost of business for sweatshops – and thus affect the capacity of sweatshops to hire and expand – and ultimately the nature of economic growth in the host country, they affect the welfare not only of current sweatshop employees but of potential sweatshop employees, employees in other industries, the families of current and potential workers, and so on.

would prefer larger paychecks to a package of smaller paychecks and safer working conditions, then laws that mandate safer working conditions will harm workers to the extent that the costs of providing those safer working conditions are paid from funds that would have otherwise been used to compensate workers directly. If adherence to minimum wage laws leads sweatshops to employ fewer workers in the poor country than they otherwise would have, then doing so will obviously set back the interests of those who will be unemployed as a result. The reason that sweatshop critics believe that adherence to labor laws is nevertheless morally obligatory is, in large part, because they do not believe that adhering to them will produce these harmful effects. But as was argued in Chapter 3, this belief is based on serious misunderstandings of economic theory and data.

Previously I argued that violating individual laws can be good for workers' welfare. Critics could respond that labor laws should be respected because "respect for the rule of law contributes to increased prosperity."[47] Thus, they may claim that although an individual law might be harmful to workers, respecting even those laws benefits workers in the long run because of the increased prosperity from abiding by the rule of law.

However, the "rule of law" that brings economic prosperity is very different from simply respecting whatever laws happen to exist in a country. When economists find that growth comes from following the rule of law, they are writing about legal systems that protect private property rights, uphold contracts, and are applied universally, predictably, and clearly.[48] Most sweatshop-containing countries do not have such legal systems, and thus following their existing laws would not lead to prosperity.

The claim that sweatshops might be morally justified in violating the law in certain cases is hardly a radical philosophical position. If any conclusion can be gleaned from the massive philosophical literature on

---

[47] Arnold and Hartman make this argument, "Beyond Sweatshops," 220.

[48] See Gwartney, James, Robert Lawson, and Joshua Hall. *Economic Freedom of the World Annual Report*. Vancouver, BC, Canada: The Fraser Institute, 2011, available at www.freetheworld.org, for much of the research that has made use of the Economic Freedom of the World Annual Report showing the types of systems that produce prosperity are those that respect negative rights and do not have highly regulated labor markets.

political authority, it is that justifying even a prima facie obligation to obey the law is a tremendously difficult, and possibly hopeless, task. Traditional accounts of political authority, as Robert Paul Wolff has argued, seem to be incompatible with a respect for individual autonomy.[49] In short, as Leslie Green writes, "There are plausible objections to each of the dominant justifications for the duty to obey the law," to an even greater degree than is present for most philosophic issues.[50] Of course, these problems plague the justification of a duty to obey even those laws that well-functioning democratic systems generate and that are neutral or even benign in their effect. How much more problematic, then, must be the justification of a duty to obey laws that are generated in an autocratic or unjust way, and which are harmful in their effects on the most vulnerable segments of the population?

CONCLUSION

Anti-sweatshop activists and scholars seem to think they have a trump card when they ask if defenders of sweatshops advocate breaking labor standards laws. Viederman writes that if you believe sweatshop jobs are good then,

> Does that mean even an illegal job? ... Ethical standards are the rule of law in almost every country in the world. Do pro-sweatshopers think that legal standards shouldn't be implemented? Where that's the case, those in power can and do claim as much of the revenue pie as they can, cheating workers out of their wages, cutting corners on worker safety, and all manner of other tactics.[51]

Yes, even an illegal job. Activists such as Viederman fail to understand the economics that determine wage levels and how wages relate to safety and other working conditions. Legal standards should not be implemented. When they are, they should be ignored. Contrary to Viederman's assertions, workers will be made better off as a result.

The issues of wage compensation and safety, comfort, and other benefits are intimately related. If activists push only to improve safety

---

[49] Robert Paul Wolff, *In Defense of Anarchism*, 3rd ed. (Berkeley: University of California Press, 1970).

[50] Leslie Green, *Legal Obligation and Authority*, October 1, 2010, retrieved from http://plato.stanford.edu/entries/legal-obligation/.

[51] Viederman, "Any Job Is a Good Job? Think Again."

in factories, then either they are implicitly pushing for a reduction in monetary wages that workers have already demonstrated they prefer more than safety, or they will unemploy workers by raising their total compensation above their marginal productivity. Profit-seeking companies will make trade-offs on these margins when activists push for reforms. These trade-offs are binding constraints, not something activists can assume away. This is why economists do not separate the analysis of safety, health, comfort, and other in-kind benefits from wages. If any of these factors raise total compensation above worker productivity, the worker will be unemployed. Alternatively, if total compensation stays the same and reformers demand improved conditions, wages will decrease. Thus, activists should not push to mandate improved working conditions in poorer countries. When these countries impose their own labor laws dictating minimum wages as well as health, safety, and working conditions, those firms that ignore the local labor laws often improve the welfare of the workers. First World activists should cease general calls to obey local labor laws and should instead focus only on those violations, such as forced labor, that actually harm the workers.

6

Save the Children?

The thought of a young child working in a Third World sweatshop is repulsive to most people. And rightly so. Consider the case of Halima.[1] She is an eleven-year-old girl who clips loose threads off of Hanes underwear in a Bangladeshi factory. She works about eight hours a day, six days per week. She has to process 150 pairs of underwear an hour. When she falls behind, supervisors shout at her or slap her. She is only allowed to go to the bathroom two or three times per day, and it does not have soap or toilet paper. At work she feels "very tired and exhausted," and sometimes falls asleep standing up. She makes 53 cents a day for her efforts.

You might understand the logic of the preceding chapters and have revised your views on the desirability of sweatshops, but there is probably a lingering fear that if we allowed the global market to determine employment without governmental regulation, we would end up with many children such as Halima working in the factories. So, some laws must be needed to save the children. Right?

Anti-sweatshop groups almost universally condemn child labor. Provisions against child labor are part of the International Labor Organization's core labor standards. However, as repulsive as child labor is, all of the analysis in preceding chapters applies to children as well as adults. We should desire to see an end to child labor, but it has to come through a process that generates better opportunities for them – not from legislative mandates that prevent children from taking the best

---

[1] The National Labor Committee interviewed Halima in 2006. A video of the interview is available online: "Child Labor: 11 year-old Halima Sews Clothing for Hanes," retrieved from http://www.youtube.com/watch?v=pTIfY9SmJdA.

option available to them. Children do not work because their parents are mean. They work because their families are desperately poor, and the meager addition to the family income they can contribute is often necessary for survival. Banning child labor through trade regulations or governmental prohibitions often simply forces the children into less-desirable alternatives. When U.S. activists started pressuring Bangladesh into eliminating child labor, the results were disastrous.

In 1993, U.S. Senator Tom Harkin introduced the Child Labor Deterrence Act, which would have banned imports from countries employing children. In response, Bangladeshi garment companies fired approximately 50,000 children that fall. According to the U.S. Department of Labor, "It is widely thought that most of them have found employment in other garment factories, in smaller, unregistered subcontracting garment workshops, or in other sectors."[2] That makes the introduction of the bill seem simply ineffective. The Department of Labor is sugarcoating it. Paul Krugman summarizes what happened more bluntly: "The direct result was that Bangladeshi textile factories stopped employing children. But did the children go back to school? Did they return to happy homes? Not according to Oxfam, which found that the displaced child workers ended up in even worse jobs, or on the streets – and that a significant number were forced into prostitution."[3] Similar to adults, and sometimes with the advice of adults, children tend to choose the job that they believe is their best available option. Taking that option away does not eliminate the necessity of work; it forces them to take a less-desirable job. As repulsive as a child working in a sweat-shop may be, it is not nearly as repulsive as a child forced into prostitution through the actions of unthinking Western activists.

The Bangladesh story is a dramatic one, but it is representative of many of the alternatives the children face.[4] We next examine the general

---

[2] U.S. Department of Labor, Bureau of International Labor Affairs, 1994 Child Labor Report, Bangladesh, retrieved from http://www.dol.gov/ilab/media/reports/iclp/sweat/bangladesh.htm.

[3] Paul Krugman, "Reckonings; Hearts and Heads," *New York Times*, April 22, 2001, 17. Similarly, the UNICEF report "The State of the World's Children," 1997, retrieved from http://www.unicef.org/sowc97/, reports that many of these children turned to prostitution.

[4] For an excellent survey of the economics and composition of child labor, see Eric Edmonds and Nina Pavcnik, "Child Labor in the Global Economy," *Journal of Economic Perspectives* 19, No. 1 (Winter 2005), 199–220.

alternatives available to children in countries where sweatshops are located. Then, we explore ways that child labor can be eliminated without throwing the children into worse alternatives.

ALTERNATIVES AVAILABLE TO CHILDREN

Implicit in the condemnation of child labor in sweatshops is an assumption that these factories have taken advantage of children who would otherwise have had better opportunities, such as attending school. But garment factories are not unique in their employment of children in these countries. In countries where sweatshops locate, child labor is often the norm, and most of the children work in less remunerative sectors with fewer opportunities for advancement than manufacturing, such as agriculture or domestic services. In 2004, the International Labor Organization copublished a series of similar national child-labor studies.[5] Among the reports were studies in El Salvador, Costa Rica, and the Dominican Republic; in all of these countries firms have been accused of being sweatshops. A look at these studies helps put child sweatshop labor into the proper perspective.

The studies examined the work and school attendance of children aged five to seventeen years old in each country. Approximately 10 percent of these children worked in Costa Rica, 18 percent in the Dominican Republic, and 12 percent in El Salvador. Low rates of work among five to nine year olds bias these numbers downward significantly. The average age of child workers was fourteen in Costa Rica and El Salvador and twelve and a half in the Dominican Republic. Although most children went to school in these countries, a significant number did not. Seven percent of Dominican children, 15 percent of Costa Rican children, and 23 percent of El Salvadorian children did not attend school.

Manufacturing, the industry in which most sweatshops would be classified, was not the dominant employer of children. In Costa Rica

---

[5] International Labor Organization, "Summary of the Results of the Child and Adolescent Labour Survey in Costa Rica," 2002; "Summary of the Results of the National Child Labour Survey in the Dominican Republic," 2000; and "Summary of the Results of the Child Labour Survey in El Salvador," 2003. All retrieved from http://www.ilo.org/ipec/ChildlabourstatisticsSIMPOC/Questionnairessurveysandreports/lang--en/index.htm.

and El Salvador, agriculture was the main occupation of most working children, at 44 and 49 percent, respectively. This was followed by trade, hotels, and restaurants, which accounted for 27 percent in Costa Rica and 23 percent in El Salvador, whereas manufacturing employed only 9 and 16 percent of children, respectively. In the Dominican Republic, the service industry was the main employer of children (41 percent), followed by trade, agriculture, and finally manufacturing.

Forms of compensation varied, but in Costa Rica and El Salvador unpaid family work was the most common form of child labor. In the Dominican Republic salaried compensation was more common. Regardless of the form of compensation or industry that the children worked in, their hours were significant. In Costa Rica and El Salvador, working children worked an average of thirty-one hours per week, and in the Dominican Republic they averaged twenty-one hours.

The ILO also examined a "child labour" population that consisted of children whose "involvement in economic activities violates national legislation and/or international agreements, because it is physically, mentally, socially, or morally harmful or detrimental to children, or because it somehow interferes with their schooling."[6] The ILO found that 65 percent of working children in Costa Rica, 80 percent in the Dominican Republic, and 50 percent in El Salvador are engaged in this sort of child labor. Manufacturing jobs were not systematically more likely to be classified as this form of child labor than other sectors. In the Dominican Republic, agriculture had the largest percentage of its jobs classified as child labor, whereas manufacturing, services, and trade each had a similar proportion. In El Salvador, the trade sector had the highest percentage of jobs classified as child labor, whereas manufacturing had the lowest proportion. In Costa Rica, 68 percent of manufacturing jobs were classified as child labor, followed closely by agriculture at 67 percent and trade at 57 percent.

The picture these reports paint is that child labor is common in these countries. Most child labor is not in the manufacturing sector, and manufacturing jobs are not systematically more likely to be classified as harmful by the ILO. How well do these cases generalize?

The World Bank's World Development Indicators report statistics on child labor. In 2003, the World Bank measured the percent of

---

[6] ILO, "Costa Rica Survey" (2002): 7.

Table 6.1 *Percent of Children Aged
Ten to Fourteen in Labor Force*

Bangladesh	26.5%
Brazil	13.4%
China	5.5%
Costa Rica	3.3%
Dominican Republic	11.5%
El Salvador	10.3%
Haiti	21.4%
Honduras	5.5%
India	10.7%
Indonesia	6.8%
Mauritius	1.4%
Burma	22.0%
Nicaragua	8.9%
Thailand	10.0%

children aged ten to fourteen that were working in most countries.[7] A look at the subset of countries where sweatshops have been reported in the press reveals that, like the above three examples, most children are not working, but that child labor is not uncommon in most of these countries. As Table 6.1 shows, rates of child labor range from a high of nearly 27 percent of children in Bangladesh to a low of 1.4 percent in Mauritius. However, as explained in Chapter 4, Mauritius is an outlier whose reported sweatshops employ immigrants.

Educational statistics are also similar to the previous case studies. In most countries where sweatshops locate, the majority of children complete primary education. Thus, despite the presence of child employment, it does not necessarily come at the expense of basic education. However, in many countries with sweatshops, a significant portion of children do not complete primary education. For example, in Bangladesh more than 40 percent of students do not complete primary education. Secondary education enrollment rates are signifi-cantly lower. In Cambodia, fewer than 23 percent of children of the appropriate age are enrolled in secondary education. Table 6.2 summarizes the primary education completion and secondary

[7] World Development Indicators CD-ROM (2005).

Table 6.2 *Child Education*

	Percent of Relevant Age Group	
	Completes Primary Ed	**Enrolled in Secondary Ed**
Bangladesh	58.6%	41.1%
Brazil		72.2%
Cambodia	61.6%	22.7%
China	95.6%	
Costa Rica	88.9%	46.1%
Dominican Republic	83.4%	50.0%
El Salvador	83.8%	51.3%
Haiti	47.1%	
Honduras	85.2%	
India	80.7%	
Indonesia		61.5%
Laos	68.8%	32.3%
Mauritius	95.4%	71.6%
Burma	87.5%	41.1%
Nicaragua	69.1%	40.9%
South Africa	90.5%	66.7%
Thailand	87.0%	68.6%
Vietnam	98.3%	60.7%

education enrollment rates for the countries where sweatshops have been reported.[8]

Although they are more limited in coverage, the World Bank also collects data on the economic sectors in which children are employed. Figure 6.1 presents the distribution of employment of economically active children between the ages of seven and fourteen by sector.[9] As in our previous case studies, the vast majority of employed children are not employed in manufacturing. In seven of the nine countries for which data exists, most children were employed in agriculture, often by a wide margin.[10] In the two exceptions, Costa Rica and the Dominican Republic, the leading sector employing children was service. El

---

[8] Rates are an average over the period from 1995 to 2009 for which data are available. Brazil and Indonesia's primary education rates are excluded because they are clearly incorrect (exceeding 100 percent).

[9] For each country, an average was taken for all years between 2000 and 2009 for which data are available.

[10] The World Bank database does not include data for Vietnam, but Edmonds and Pavcnik, "Child Labor in the Global Economy," report that 92 percent of children working in Vietnam in 1998 worked in agriculture.

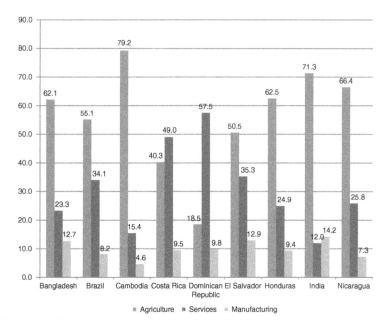

Figure 6.1 Percent of economically active children employed by sector.

Salvador had the highest proportion of children employed in manufacturing, and there it was just less than 13 percent.

Protests against sweatshops that use child labor or trade sanctions such as the Child Labor Deterrence Act assume that ending child labor in sweatshops by taking away the option to work in a factory will, on net, reduce child labor. Evidence on child labor in countries that have sweatshops indicates that they are wrong. It is not a few "bad apple" firms exploiting children in factories. Child labor is common. Moreover, sweatshops and manufacturing are not where most children work. Most work in agriculture or service sector jobs. These other sectors are not necessarily safer, either. Child-labor surveys show that 12 percent of children working in agriculture report injuries, compared with 9 percent of those who work in manufacturing.[11] If children lose their jobs in export manufacturing, the alternative for most is not some comfortable time in school but another job in a lower-growth, lower-skill sector of the economy. Similar to their adult counterparts, we do not help Third World children by taking options away from them; we help them only when

---

[11] Kebebew Asshagrie, *Statistics on Working Children and Hazardous Child Labour in Brief* (Geneva: International Labor Office, 1997).

their options are expanded. Chapter 9 will discuss some marginal differences activists could make in expanding their options, but the next section of this chapter explains the main way that child labor is eradicated.

ECONOMIC DEVELOPMENT AND CHILD LABOR

The thought of Third World children toiling in factories to produce garments for us in the developed world to wear is appalling, at least in part because child labor is virtually nonexistent in the United States and the rest of the more developed world.[12] Sure, some kids have chores to do around the house, others might have a paper route, and high school aged kids might have a part-time job. But virtually nowhere in the developed world do kids toil long hours every week in a factory or on the family farm in a manner that prevents them from obtaining schooling.

This pleasant situation is taken for granted by many in wealthy countries. But it is not the norm historically. Children typically worked throughout human history, either long hours in agriculture or in factories once the industrial revolution emerged. The question is, why don't kids work today? A tempting answer would be because the United States and other wealthy countries have laws against child labor. But that answer would be wrong.

Rich countries do have laws against child labor, but so do many poor countries. In Costa Rica, the legal working age is fifteen, but the ILO survey found 43 percent of working children were under the legal age. Similarly, in the United States, Massachusetts passed the first restriction on child labor in 1842. However, that law and other states' laws affected child labor nationally very little.[13] By one estimate, more than 25 percent of males between the ages of ten and fifteen participated in the labor force in 1900.[14] Another study of both boys and girls

---

[12] The ILO estimates that 18 percent of children aged five to fourteen are economically active worldwide. Of these, it estimates that 94 percent of them are in low-income countries, and only 2 percent are in what it classifies as developed countries. ILO, *Every Child Counts: New Global Estimates on Child Labour* (Geneva: ILO, 2002).

[13] The remainder of this paragraph and the next draw on research found in Joshua Hall and Peter Leeson, "Good for the Goose, Bad for the Gander: International Labor Standards and Comparative Development," *Journal of Labor Research* 28, No. 4 (September 2007), 658–676.

[14] R. Whaples, "Child Labor in the United States," in EH.Net Encyclopedia, ed. R. Whaples, retrieved from http://eh.net/encyclopedia/article/whaples.childlabor.

in that age group estimated that more than 18 percent of them were employed in 1900.[15] Carolyn Moehling also found little evidence that minimum-age laws for manufacturing implemented between 1880 and 1910 contributed to the decline in child labor.[16] Claudia Goldin and Larry Katz examined the period between 1910 and 1939 and found that child labor laws and compulsory school-attendance laws could explain at most 5 percent of the increase in high school enrollment.[17] The United States did not enact a national law limiting child labor until the Fair Labor Standards Act was passed in 1938. By that time, the U.S. average per capita income was more than $10,200.00 (in 2010 dollars), a level far above that of most of the sweatshop countries analyzed here.

Furthermore, child labor was defined much more narrowly when today's wealthy countries first prohibited it. Massachusetts's law limited children who were under twelve years old to no more than ten hours of work per day. This is hardly a restriction at all. Belgium (1886) and France (1847) prohibited only children under the age of twelve from working. Germany (1891) set the minimum working age at thirteen.[18] England, which passed its first enforceable child labor law in 1833, really did not have much of a restriction at all. The law merely set the minimum age for textile work at nine years old. When these countries were developing, they simply did not put in place the type of restrictions on child labor that activists demand for Third World countries today. Binding legal restrictions came only after child labor had mostly disappeared.

The main reason children do not work in the United States and other wealthy countries is precisely *because* they are wealthy. Although many parents may think a little part-time work for a child helps instill a good work ethic, few desire to see their children work in risky jobs or jobs that would totally eliminate their play or get in the way of their education and future development. The same is true of

---

[15] Samuel Lindsay, "Child Labor in the United States," *American Economic Association* 8 (February 1907), 256–259.

[16] Carolyn Moehling, "State Child Labor Laws and the Decline in Child Labor," *Explorations in Economic History* 36, No. 1 (1999), 72–105.

[17] Claudia Goldin and Larry Katz, "Mass Secondary Schooling and the State: The Role of State Compulsion and the High School Movement," *NBER Working Paper* No. 10075 (2003).

[18] France and Prussia both had earlier laws prohibiting child labor, but they were not enforceable. See Hall and Leeson, "Good for the Goose," 658–676.

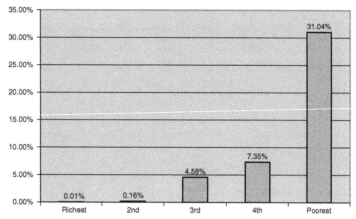

Figure 6.2 Percent of children aged ten to fourteen in labor force by country income quintile.

most Third World parents. Their problem is that they are poor and need their children's incomes to help feed and clothe the family.

The relationship between child labor and income is striking. Using the same World Bank data on child labor participation rates from Table 6.1, we can observe how child labor varies with per capita income. Figure 6.2 divides countries into five groups based on their level of per capita income adjusted for purchasing power parity. In the richest fifth of countries, all of whose incomes exceed $24,000.00 in 2010 dollars, child labor is virtually nonexistent. In the second-richest fifth of countries, with per capita incomes ranging from $12,000.00 to $24,000.00, child labor is also virtually nonexistent.

It is only when countries have an income less than $11,000.00 per year that we start to observe children in the labor force. But even here, rates of child labor remain relatively low through both the third and fourth quintiles. It is really the poorest countries where rates of child labor explode. More than 30 percent of children work in the fifth of countries with incomes ranging from $600.00 to $2,000.00 per year. Eric Edmonds and Nina Pavcnik econometrically estimate that 73 percent of the variation of child labor rates can be explained by variation in GDP per capita.[19]

---

[19] Edmonds and Pavcnik, "Child Labor in the Global Economy," 210.

Of course, correlation is not causation. But in the case of child labor and wealth, the most intuitive interpretation is that increased wealth leads to reduced child labor. After all, all countries were once poor; in the countries that became rich, child labor disappeared. Few would contend that child labor disappeared in the United States or Great Britain prior to economic growth taking place – children populated their factories much as they do in the Third World today. A little introspection, or for that matter our moral indignation at Third World child labor, reveals that most of us desire that children, especially our own, do not work. Thus, as we become richer and can afford to allow children to have leisure and education, we choose to.

Scholars have debated these points, however. Some have claimed that child labor might impede the formation of human capital, reducing economic growth and thus trapping countries in poverty.[20] If child labor caused poverty, it would beg the question of how most countries have virtually eliminated child labor. They all once used child labor; how did so many escape the trap? Furthermore, in all but the poorest quintile, less than 10 percent of children work. Why would the impediment to human capital formation of 10 percent of children prevent the other 90 percent of children from gaining human capital and causing economic development? Also, working is not necessarily incompatible with school attendance. In 2000 and 2001, UNICEF surveyed thirty-six low-income countries on their use of child labor. They found that almost 74 percent of children aged five to fourteen who worked also attended school.[21] As economists Eric Edmonds and Nina Pavcnik report, for those children who do sacrifice school for work, domestic work is at least as likely to crowd out schooling as manufacturing jobs.[22]

The overall cross-country empirical evidence in the economics literature suggests a strong link between the level of income and

---

[20] For a couple of examples, see Kaushik Basu, "Child Labor: Cause, Consequence, and Cure, with Remarks on International Labor Standards," *Journal of Economic Literature* 37, No. 3 (September 1999), 1083–1119; and Christopher Heady, "The Effect of Child Labor on Learning Achievement," *World Development* 31, No. 3 (2003), 385–398.

[21] Edmonds and Pavcnik, "Child Labor in the Global Economy," 205.

[22] Edmonds and Pavcnik, "Child Labor in the Global Economy," 204.

elimination of child labor.[23] So does the history of the many countries that have developed.[24] But some single-country, cross-sectional household survey research fails to find a strong link between a family's income and whether children work.[25] There are two interpretations for this. One is that cultural norms may lead parents in some countries to not view child labor as a bad thing, and thus rising incomes will not reduce child labor. The other explanation is that higher incomes could result in more profitable opportunities for children to work and thus entice them away from school and leisure.

Both of these explanations are plausible, but another study points to a bigger problem. The single-country studies of income and child labor may not find a statistically significant relationship between the two because their empirical techniques are flawed. The studies looked for a general and uniform decrease in child labor as household income increased. However, a family that is below the poverty line may see its income increase but still need children to work because it remains below the poverty line. Similarly, wealthier families may not change the number of children working (if any) because they were already well above the poverty line. If changes in child labor are clustered around the poverty line, the statistical techniques of the household-level studies would likely fail to pick them up.[26]

Child labor studies that track family income over time almost universally find large declines in child labor when incomes increase.[27] Let us look at one of these studies in detail. An important study of child labor in Vietnam, a country where sweatshops have been reported,

---

[23] For example, see Alan Krueger, "International Labor Standards and Trade," in *Annual World Bank Conference on Development Economics* 1996, eds. M. Bruno and B. Pleskovic (Washington DC: The World Bank, 1997), 281–302.

[24] See Moehling, "State Child Labor Laws," 72–106.

[25] For a survey, see Drusilla Brown, Alan Deardorff, and Robert Stern, "Child Labor: Theory, Evidence and Policy," in *International Labor Standards: History, Theories and Policy*, eds. K. Basu et al. (Oxford: Basil Blackwell, 2003).

[26] In more technical terms, the studies were looking for a linear relationship between child labor and income, but there might be a strong nonlinear relationship between the two that these techniques would fail to discover if they were averaging child labor over data ranges in which child labor is and is not elastic. Instead, nonparametric techniques are needed.

[27] Edmonds and Pavcnik, "Child Labor in the Global Economy," 211.

addresses the empirical shortcoming raised here.[28] Between 1993 and 1997, Vietnam averaged 9 percent GDP growth, and child labor declined 30 percent. Economist Eric Edmonds used survey data that tracked individual households' expenditures and whether children aged six to fifteen worked over a period of five years. Because he was tracking individual households over time, differences in rates of child labor as the economy grew cannot be explained by differences in family preferences or cultural norms, as those are held constant.

Importantly, he looked for changes in child labor as expenditures grew around poverty lines rather than for general changes. He specifically looked at how child labor changed when household expenditures moved from below what was necessary to supply a 2,100-calorie daily diet to above ($65.00 per year), and when expenditures moved above the official poverty line ($106.00 per year). In 1993, 25 percent of the population had expenditures below what it takes to satisfy a 2,100-calorie diet. That number had fallen to 8 percent by 1998. In 1993, 58 percent of the households were below the official poverty line, but by 1998 only 33 percent of households were below the 1993 line.

How did these changes correlate with child labor? For households whose expenditures rose but remained below what is necessary to sustain a 2,100-calorie diet, very little. After all, these families remained desperately poor and likely still needed their children to work. However, around the 2,100-calorie level, child labor begins to decline as expenditures rise. Then, the decline in child labor accelerates as expenditures rise to the official poverty line. For the overall sample, Edmonds finds that child labor declines as expenditures increase, but the real action is around the poverty level. For households that emerged from poverty during the period, the increase in expenditure explains 80 percent of the decrease in child labor.[29]

This study of household-level data in Vietnam corrects for the statistical problems in other household-level research. The finding is consistent with the cross-country evidence that implies when a country becomes wealthier child labor will decrease. It also squares with common sense.

---

[28] Eric Edmonds, "Does Child Labor Decline with Improving Economic Status?" *Journal of Human Resources* 40, No. 1 (2005), 77–99.

[29] Edmonds's results point to the importance of using nonlinear techniques. Although his method picked up 80 percent of the decline in child labor for groups emerging from poverty, linear techniques pick up only 51 percent of the decline.

CONCLUSION

The thought of children laboring in sweatshops is even more repulsive than the thought of adults laboring in them. But that does not mean we can simply "think" with our hearts and not our heads. Adults who choose to work in sweatshops do so because they are poor and it is the best available alternative open to them. The same is true of children, who often come from even poorer families than the adults who work in sweatshops. The vast majority of children employed in countries with sweatshops work in lower-productivity sectors than manufacturing. Passing trade sanctions or other laws that take away the option of children working in sweatshops only limits their options further and throws them into these other industries or even worse alternatives. Luckily, as families escape poverty, child labor declines. As countries become rich, child labor virtually disappears. The answer for how to cure child labor is the same as the one for how to improve the lives of adult sweatshop workers. It lies in the process of economic growth – a process in which sweatshops play an important role.

7

Is It Ethical to Buy Sweatshop Products?

The standard economic defense of sweatshops holds that sweatshop jobs should not be jeopardized because they are better than the other alternatives workers face. Is that enough to make it ethical for companies to offer jobs with such low pay and poor working conditions, and for us to buy their products? Economist Ludwig Von Mises made a moral claim that many economists, who have defended sweatshops, have implicitly endorsed his defense of factory owners of the industrial revolution, writing: "It is deplorable that such [impoverished] conditions existed [outside the factories]. But if one wants to blame those responsible, one must not blame the factory owners who – driven by selfishness, of course, and not by 'altruism' – did all they could to eradicate the evils. What had caused these evils was the economic order of the precapitalistic era."[1] Is he right that firms are not blameworthy for taking advantage of the poverty caused by the prior economic order? The poverty that leads workers to choose sweatshops today is often caused by background injustices that are not the direct fault of the firm. This raises many important ethical questions.

Are we unfairly exploiting sweatshop workers when we buy products made with their labor? Do we benefit a great deal whereas they get only a pittance? Many people experience moral outrage when others buy products made in sweatshops, but that same moral outrage is seldom directed at those who do not give charitably to impoverished subsistence farmers throughout the world. Why? The subsistence farmers are often poorer and more in need of our help. By trading with sweatshop workers, do we take on a moral responsibility to do

[1] Ludwig Von Mises, *Human Action*, 1949 (Auburn: Ludwig Von Mises Institute, 1998), 615.

something more for them than the responsibility we have to other poor
people with whom we do not trade? If the lack of good alternatives
is the result of grave injustices, are people who deal with sweatshop
workers obligated to try to correct these injustices? These ethical
concerns are important because they may lead you to feel "dirty" for
buying sweatshop products even if you believe the economic arguments in the preceding chapters.

IS IT WRONGFUL EXPLOITATION?

A number of academics have argued that sweatshops are wrongfully
exploitative.[2] Philosophers dispute what exactly it means to be exploited;
my purpose is not to try to resolve that dispute.[3] Most accounts, however,
hold that wrongful exploitation consists of taking advantage of another
person in a way that is either unfair or that fails to manifest sufficient
respect for that person's dignity. An interaction can be both voluntary
and beneficial to both parties (relative to how they would have fared in
the absence of any interaction) and still be wrongfully exploitative.

[2] See, for instance, Denis Arnold and Norman Bowie, "Sweatshops and Respect for
Persons," *Business Ethics Quarterly* 13, No. 2 (April 2003), 221–242; Robert Mayer,
"Sweatshops, Exploitation, and Moral Responsibility," *Journal of Social Philosophy*
38, No. 4 (2007), 605–619; Chris Meyers, "Wrongful Beneficence: Exploitation and
Third World Sweatshops," *Journal of Social Philosophy* 35, No. 3 (2004), 319–333;
Jeremy C. Snyder, "Needs Exploitation," *Ethical Theory and Moral Practice*, 11, No. 4
(2008), 389–405; Jeremy C. Snyder, "Exploitation and Sweatshop Labor: Perspectives
and Issues," *Business Ethics Quarterly* 20, No. 2 (April 2010), 187–213; and Iris
Marion Young, "Responsibility and Global Justice: A Social Connection Model,"
Social Philosophy and Policy 23, No. 1 (January 2006), 102–130.

[3] Some of the most influential accounts include Robert E. Goodin, "Exploiting a Situation
and Exploiting a Person," in *Modern Theories of Exploitation*, ed. Andrew Reeve
(London: Sage, 1987), 166–200; Allen W. Wood, "Exploitation," *Social Philosophy and
Policy* 12, No. 2 (1995), 136–158; Alan Wertheimer, *Exploitation* (Princeton: Princeton
University Press, 1996); Ruth Sample, *Exploitation: What It Is and Why It's Wrong*
(New York: Rowman and Littlefield, 2003); Robert Mayer, "What's Wrong with
Exploitation?" *Journal of Applied Philosophy* 24, No. 2 (2007), 137–150;
Mikhail Valdman, "Exploitation and Injustice," *Social Theory and Practice: An
International and Interdisciplinary Journal of Social Philosophy* 34, No. 4 (October
2008), 551–572; and Mikhail Valdman, "A Theory of Wrongful Exploitation,"
Philosophers' Imprint 9 No. 6 (July 2009), 1–14. Wertheimer, *Exploitation*, available at
http://plato.stanford.edu/archives/fall2008/entries/exploitation/, January 12, 2010, provides an overview of most of the main philosophical accounts. Snyder, "Exploitation
and Sweatshop Labor," provides another overview with specific focus on the application
of such accounts to the issue of sweatshop labor.

Suppose, for example, that a boater offers to rescue a drowning man by selling him a spot on the boat for $10,000.00, and the drowning man accepts the offer. The deal is clearly beneficial to the boater – I assume he values the $10,000.00 much more highly than the time and effort he must sacrifice – and it is no less clearly beneficial to the drowning man. The drowning man surely values his life more highly than the $10,000.00 he had to give up to save it. If he did not, he would not have accepted the boater's offer. Still, most people (including myself) would judge that the boater has acted wrongly in making his rescue contingent upon paying such an exorbitant sum. In doing so, the boater seems to be taking wrongful advantage of his monopoly on the means of rescue and failing to treat the drowning man with the respect he deserves.

Can sweatshop labor be analyzed in a similar way? Perhaps potential sweatshop workers are like people drowning in lakes, and the multinational enterprises (MNEs) that ultimately finance their employment are like the boater. The potential workers are in a desperate situation, "drowning" in poverty and perhaps unable to adequately provide for themselves and their families. MNEs have power in the form of wealth to rescue these individuals. But rather than providing that rescue out of common kindness or a sense of moral obligation, they make it contingent on an onerous payment. The MNE will provide the worker with just enough money to make the employment offer attractive, and will demand in exchange that the worker toil for long hours in dangerous and unpleasant conditions. Such an offer might present the worker with a better alternative than anything else she has available, but so does the boater's offer, and this does not make it any less unfair, demeaning, or objectionable.

There are good reasons for thinking that the standard cases of sweatshop labor – even those involving low wages and very bad working conditions – are not wrongfully exploitative. First, it is not clear that the distribution of burdens and benefits between sweatshop workers and MNEs is unfair, and hence that MNEs are taking unfair advantage of sweatshop workers. Part of the problem in credibly establishing the charge of unfairness stems from the immense difficulty in specifying a general principle of fair distribution, something no critic of sweatshops has yet managed to do. Even without such a principle, of course, critics of sweatshops might hold that the division is unfair in some obvious and intuitive way – perhaps because MNEs are clearly getting more than they ought to out of the transaction or because workers are clearly getting less. But neither of the factual claims on which this "obvious and intuitive" account of unfairness rests is accurate. The rate of profit in MNEs that outsource is generally no higher than it is in other industries with a similar level of risk. The oft-cited fact that a sweatshop worker who produces, say, a pair of Nike shoes is paid only $1.00 to make a pair of shoes that sells for around $100.00 does not mean that Nike is walking away from the exchange with $99.00 and the worker with only $1.00.[4] Most of the $100.00 goes to paying for advertising, retailer mark up, raw materials, transportation costs, and so on. The amount that actually accrues to Nike as profit is generally no greater as a percentage of their investment than the profits in any other competitive industry. Thus, MNEs are not earning unusually high profits off the backs of sweatshop workers. Nor is it obvious that sweatshop workers are receiving less than they ought to earn in wages. Such a claim might be credible if MNEs were, as some critics have charged, utilizing their monopsonistic power to pay workers less than the market rate for their labor. But as I argued in Chapter 3, there is no reason to think that workers' wages are not determined, by and large, by their productivity – just as the wages of non-sweatshop workers are.

Let us put dollars and cents aside for a moment and think about how trading with sweatshop workers impacts lives. The small amount of pay they receive often represents a large improvement in their ability to feed, clothe, and shelter their families. The slightly cheaper shirt for a consumer in the United States or the little bit of extra profit the sweatshop employee generates for a corporation makes a trivial difference in our lives. In fact, a T-shirt could capture this point nicely. It would have a sweatshop worker on the front with a caption that says "She fed and clothed her family" and the back of the shirt would read, "and all I got is this lousy T-shirt." Thought of this way, it is the sweatshop workers who are getting the lion's share of the total benefits from their interaction with U.S. firms. Unfortunately, we have no objective way to measure and compare these gains, but it is these gains that are really important – not just the dollars and cents we can measure.

The problem stems from the fact that economists have long recognized that there is no way to measure cardinal utility (happiness) or

---

[4] This particular version of the claim is taken from Meyers, "Wrongful Beneficence," 331.

make interpersonal comparisons of utility. Instead, economists typically measure wealth maximization in dollars. Wealth maximization maps to utility maximization only with the unrealistic assumption that a dollar generates an equal amount of happiness (utility) no matter who gets it. This is particularly relevant for sweatshop workers who have little wealth relative to Western investors and consumers. There may be no way to measure it, but intuitively, in most cases an extra dollar for a sweatshop worker generates more happiness for him than an extra dollar for a typical U.S. investor or consumer. Thus, even if U.S. citizens benefited more in dollar terms from trade with sweatshop workers, it is unlikely that U.S. citizens benefited more in terms of utility.

The charge of unfairness, and hence of exploitation, seems to derive some traction in the comparison drawn between sweatshops and the boat-rescue case described previously. But on closer examination, these cases are dissimilar in ways that are morally significant. First, part of what drives our intuition in the rescue case is the belief that the boat owner will not be made significantly worse off by performing the rescue for free. However, as argued in earlier chapters, increases in sweatshop wages or improvements in employees' working conditions will come at a cost to someone – if not to the employer, then to potential workers. Moreover, the rescue in the example I provided is entirely fortuitous. The boat owner just happened to be there when the victim needed rescuing. Our intuitions might be different if the boat owner were there precisely because he anticipated that people might need rescuing, especially if his being there required significant investment of time and capital. With this contrast in mind, sweatshops look less like cases of fortuitous rescue and more like cases of professional rescuers who acquire the skills and machinery to rescue people only because they expect to get paid. Absent the expected pay, there would be no rescue at all.

BACKGROUND INJUSTICE

Even if sweatshops are not guilty of providing their workers with less compensation than they should, it is still possible that workers' income is lower than it ought to be. The claim that MNEs do not exploit sweatshop workers is entirely compatible with the claim that sweatshop workers are suffering grievous injustice, and with it the claim that the income of sweatshop workers is lower than it would otherwise be as a result of this injustice.

The explanation for this paradoxical claim lies in the fact that the labor agreements between sweatshops and their employees are a product of a wide variety of factors, many of which fall well outside the responsibility of multinational enterprises. The background political and economic institutions of the host country, for instance, shape and constrain the opportunities available to potential sweatshop workers. To the extent that those institutions erect barriers to entry to new businesses, deny workers the freedom to voluntarily organize collectively, fail to protect private property, and deny people economic freedom, workers' opportunities to advance their interests and the interests of their families will be severely limited.[5] Workers' opportunities are further restricted by injustices in the global economic order, including the unjust seizure of land and natural resources by states and other entities as well as the unjust restriction of free access to Western markets by various forms of protectionism.[6] The more limited their opportunities are as a result of these injustices the more likely it is that an offer of sweatshop labor will be workers' most attractive option.

Sometimes MNEs themselves bear partial responsibility for the unjust background conditions against which labor agreements are formed. Because of the benefits that MNEs can bring to host countries, especially in the form of increased tax revenue, they are often well positioned to influence the behavior of the host-country government. MNEs can make their economic investment in a country contingent upon the government's willingness to use its power to secure special benefits for the MNE – benefits that can come at the cost of the MNE's competitors as well as the country's workers and citizens. These benefits might consist of limitations on other firms entering, seizure of land, or bans on workers voluntarily bargaining collectively. To the extent that MNEs influence governments to act unjustly in a way that constrains workers' options,

---

[5] I defend workers' freedom to organize collectively voluntarily, which is distinct from laws that allow labor unions to organize workers where a subset of all workers has the legal right to bargain collectively for all workers even when some workers and the employer would rather bargain individually. I support the law allowing collective bargaining but not the law requiring people who don't wish to bargain collectively to participate.

[6] For the story of many modern unjust land seizures, see Fred Pearce, *The Land Grabbers: The New Fight Over Who Owns the Earth* (Boston: Beacon Press, 2012).

MNEs do bear moral responsibility for the background conditions against which labor agreements are made. In this case, however, the real wrong of which MNEs are guilty is a form of joint coercion with the government rather than exploitation, per se. Going back to our boating-rescue analogy, this joint coercion would be equivalent to booby trapping someone's boat so that it will sink and they will need to be rescued. The booby trapping is wrong independent of any price offered for rescue.

More often, however, limiting background conditions are not the result of any injustice assignable to MNEs. Sometimes the main constraint on workers' options is a poverty that is due not to any positive evil but rather to the absence of the delicate combination of social, political, and institutional factors needed for the production of wealth and economic development. At times we forget that the natural standard of living throughout most of human history has been one of poverty. Until a society discovers and adopts that combination of factors, poverty with few options is the norm.

Often, the background injustices are perpetrated by the workers' own governments. Consider what has happened in Indonesia. Ever since Jeff Ballinger's campaign against Nike in the early 1990s, Indonesia has been a target for anti-sweatshop activism. The sweatshop jobs in Indonesia attract workers because they are better than the available alternatives, but many of the alternatives to sweatshops have been unjustly destroyed by companies in cooperation with the Indonesian government. For instance, in the Riau province on the large island of Sumatra, the people held forest land in common and depended on the forests for their livelihood for centuries.[7] But nearly fifty years ago President Suharto said that customary land rights were not going to be respected, and declared, "the forestlands of his sprawling nation of a thousand islands to be 'state forest.' They were to be deployed in the name of national development."[8] Journalist Fred Pearce reports that in practice, this "meant they would be handed out to anyone with the cash and the connections."[9] Frequently, that meant paper and plywood mill owners. Riau was 80 percent jungle in the late 1980s; today it is down to 30 percent. The local villagers are displaced as their land is seized and clear cut. Mursyid

---

[7] Facts in this paragraph are from Pearce, *The Land Grabbers*, 2012, 165–168.
[8] Pearce, *The Land Grabbers*, 167.
[9] Ibid.

Table 7.1 *Economic Freedom*

	Score	Rank
Bangladesh	6.17	103
Brazil	6.19	102
Burma	4.16	140
Cambodia	NA	NA
China	6.43	92
Costa Rica	7.17	41
Dominican Republic	6.68	78
El Salvador	7.15	43
Haiti	6.84	67
Honduras	7.06	51
India	6.4	94
Indonesia	6.5	84
Laos	NA	NA
Mauritius	7.67	9
Nicaragua	6.82	69
South Africa	6.49	87
Thailand	6.87	65
Vietnam	6.48	88

Source: Economic Freedom of the World 2011 Annual Report.

Muhammad Ali, a village head, described the situation: "We have no means of living here now. People are leaving to get jobs elsewhere."[10] Sometimes that elsewhere is in a sweatshop. But note: it is not the sweatshops causing the injustice. The property rights were violated by the Indonesian government and sold to lumber companies.

The governments of the countries where sweatshops locate systematically violate the economic freedoms and property rights of their citizens. Table 7.1 contains the Economic Freedom scores and rankings of the countries where sweatshops have been reported in the popular press.

The index ranks 141 countries based on scores between 1 and 10. The average country with sweatshops reported in popular news sources scores only 6.6 and would rank the seventy-sixth freest country in the world (dropping Mauritius from the sample causes the average rank to fall to eighty-seventh). For comparison, the United States

[10] Pearce, *The Land Grabbers*, 166.

scores a full point higher and ranks tenth in the index, whereas Hong Kong tops the rankings with a score of nine. The governments in these sweatshop-using countries discourage business creation and investment by taxing away profits, regulating opportunities out of existence, tampering with their currencies, limiting the ability to trade with foreigners, and failing to protect property rights. The violation of these economic freedoms is one reason why these countries are poor and workers find sweatshops are their best option.

Some left-leaning libertarians are critical of a defense of sweatshops such as the one outlined in this book because the world is not a truly free market economy.[11] I fully recognize that we do not live in a free market economy that is devoid of current and prior injustices. Some countries, such as the United States, are relatively freer than others. Sweatshop countries, by and large, have many more injustices and a greater lack of freedom.

However, although there are prior injustices and governments fail to respect peoples' freedoms, as long as the labor agreements between workers and sweatshops are not plagued by any form of procedural wrongdoing such as deception or coercion and the sweatshops are not actively perpetuating the background injustices, it is difficult to see how the claim that sweatshops are taking unfair advantage of workers can be maintained. They are taking advantage, to be sure, but they are doing so by entering into an agreement with workers that is mutually beneficial relative to their antecedent circumstances. Although sweatshop workers might reasonably wish that their antecedent circumstances were better and hence that their bargaining power with sweatshops was stronger, it is far from obvious that they have any grounds for complaint against sweatshops in circumstances such as those that we have described here. Their complaint is against their own governments. I join them in protest of these injustices and explore how activism

---

[11] See, for example, Gary Chartier, "Sweatshops, Labor Rights, and Competitive Advantage," *Oregon Review of International Law* 10, No. 1 (September 2008), 149–188; Kevin Carson, "Vulgar Libertarianism," Mutualist Blog: Free Market Anti-Capitalism, January 11, 2005, retrieved from http://mutualist.blogspot.com/2005/01/vulgar-libertarianism-watch-part-1.html; and Michael Kleen, "Sweatshops and Social Justice: Can Compassionate Libertarians Agree?" Center for a Stateless Society, November 17, 2011, retrieved from http://c4ss.org/content/8840.

might address the injustices in Chapter 10. But first we must examine whether companies have a moral duty to do more because of these injustices.

DO WE ACQUIRE GREATER OBLIGATIONS TO HELP BY TRADING WITH SWEATSHOP WORKERS?

A complaint that sweatshops are wrongfully exploiting workers because of the background injustices could be grounded only in the claim that sweatshops, or more plausibly the MNEs with which they contract, have some kind of moral obligation to rectify the injustice of the background conditions against which labor contracts are formed. Or at least to try to "correct" for this background injustice in some way when forming labor agreements with workers – perhaps by entering only into agreements of the sort that would have been formed had background conditions not been unjust.[12] This way of understanding what a non-exploitative transaction requires seems to place an unduly heavy burden on those interacting with the victims of background injustice.[13] Why should MNEs bear special responsibility for rectifying injustices for which they were not responsible?[14]

Philosopher Alan Wertheimer suggests that what he calls the "interaction principle" underlies some objections to exploitation. The interaction principle holds that "one has special responsibilities to those with whom one interacts beneficially that one would not have if one had chosen not to interact with them."[15] Along these lines, philosopher Jeremy Snyder has argued that MNEs' special obligation has its origin in

---

[12] The suggestion of entering into only those agreements that would have emerged with just background conditions is impossible to operationalize. First World companies and workers suffer from many injustices as well as Third World Workers. Absent a market process that reveals everyone's choices in the absence of injustices, there is no way to know what the actual market outcomes would be. This is one implication of the calculation and knowledge problems outlined by Ludwig Von Mises (1920, 1990) and Friedrich Hayek (1945).

[13] Wertheimer, *Exploitation*, 234.

[14] The argument that follows is closely related to one made by Matt Zwolinski "Structural Exploitation," *Social Philosophy and Policy* 29, No. 1 (Winter 2012), 154–179.

[15] Alan Wertheimer, "Matt Zwolinski's 'Choosing Sweatshops': A commentary." Unpublished manuscript, presented at the Arizona Current Research Workshop in Tuscon, AZ, January (2005).

a Kantian duty of beneficence.[16] Part of what it means to respect other persons as ends in themselves, according to this line of reasoning, is not to merely refrain from interfering with their actions but make some of their ends our own. This duty of beneficence has an imperfect form, meaning that individuals have "considerable leeway in determining when and where to direct their resources toward supporting" the autonomy of others.[17] But Snyder's key move, following the interaction principle, is to argue that when we enter into certain forms of special relationships with others, this general duty takes on a "perfect, strict form."[18] MNEs that enter into relationships with particular sweatshop employees have a special obligation of beneficence toward those employees. Because they are in a direct relationship with other human beings in desperate need, they no longer have the leeway they once had in determining how to discharge their duty of beneficence. Rather, "they are required to cede as much of their benefit from the interaction to their employees as is reasonably possible toward the end of their employees achieving a decent minimum standard of living."[19]

But there is something puzzling about Snyder's position. As we have seen, sweatshop labor generally represents a more attractive option than any other option available to workers. By making such labor opportunities available, MNEs confer considerable benefit upon their workers. Why should the very act of providing such a benefit impose upon MNEs a moral obligation to confer an even greater benefit? Why does providing some help to workers in the developing world confer an obligation to help more, especially when those who provide no help are (by Snyder's account) guilty of no moral wrongdoing? This violates a position known as the "non-worseness principle" that philosopher Matt Zwolinski has frequently defended.[20] The non-worseness principle

---

[16] See Snyder, "Needs Exploitation," 389–405; and "Exploitation and Sweatshop Labor," 187–213.

[17] Snyder, "Needs Exploitation," 396.

[18] Snyder, "Needs Exploitation," 390.

[19] Snyder, "Needs Exploitation," 396.

[20] See Zwolinski, "Sweatshops, Choice, and Exploitation," *Business Ethics Quarterly* 17, No. 4 (October 2007), 708–710; Matt Zwolinski, "The Ethics of Price Gouging," *Business Ethics Quarterly* 18, No. 3 (2008), 357–360; and Matt Zwolinski, "Price Gouging, Non-Worseness, and Distributive Justice," *Business Ethics Quarterly* 19, No. 2 (April 2009), 295–306. Jeremy C. Snyder has responded in "Efficiency, Equality, and Price Gouging: A Response to Zwolinski," *Business Ethics Quarterly* 19, No. 2 (April 2009), 303–306.

holds that it cannot be morally worse for two people to interact than to not interact at all if (1) both parties benefit from the interaction, (2) both parties consent to the interaction, and (3) the interaction does not have negative effects on others. For example, consider the following two companies:

Outsource Company: This company, based in the United States, outsources production to a poorer country. The wages it pays are considerably higher than the wages paid elsewhere in that country, and workers' lives are greatly improved by the benefits those wages confer. Moreover, the company uses a portion of the profits it earns to fund various charitable causes in its home country. It does not, however, give to its sweatshop workers as much "as is reasonably possible."

Domestic Company: This company, based in the United States, does not outsource production at all. It does, however, use a portion of its profits to fund various charitable causes in its home country.

Let us stipulate that both companies give enough to charity to satisfy an imperfect duty of beneficence. Snyder's account nevertheless implies that Outsource Company is acting wrongly, whereas Domestic Company is not.[21] This implication would seem to hold even if workers in the poor country in which Outsource Company hires workers stand in greater need of aid than the beneficiaries of the charitable causes that both companies fund. According to Snyder, the perfect nature of Outsource Company's obligations toward its employees is not a function of their need but rather of their interaction with the company. This seems implausible.

Suppose Snyder's account is right, that a company's entering into an employment relationship with a needy individual is sufficient to generate a strict, perfect duty of beneficence on the part of the company

---

I don't find his response persuasive, but it is beyond this chapter to set out a full defense of the non-worseness claim, although see Matt Zwolinski, "Exploitation and Neglect" (San Diego: University of San Diego, Department of Philosophy, 2012), for an attempt to do this.

[21] Alternatively, Snyder could hold that Outsource Company is guilty of exploitation, whereas Domestic Company is not, but that Domestic Company is guilty of some other and perhaps more serious form of moral offense. This would save Snyder's account from having to embrace the counterintuitive claim that Outsource Company is acting in a worse way than Domestic Company, but only at the price of reducing the moral significance of exploitation.

toward that employee.[22] Suppose compliance with such a duty would require the company to pay its employees at least $5.00 per hour. But let us suppose that the employer is only willing to provide its employees with $3.00 per hour. Would it be permissible, on Snyder's account, for the employer to make its offer of employment contingent upon its workers' willingness to waive their right to $5.00 per hour? Prior to entering into a relationship with employees, the employer has only an imperfect duty of beneficence. No prospective employee has any valid moral claim upon its assistance. Thus, the company would not be acting wrongly if it refused to hire or assist the prospective employee at all. If it is permissible for the employer not to hire prospective workers, and if hiring prospective workers at $3.00 per hour is better for both the employer and the worker than not hiring the prospective worker at all, then how could doing so be wrong? If, on one hand, employees' claim to a wage of at least $5.00 per hour is waivable, then employers are not necessarily acting wrongly in providing their employees with $3.00 per hour. If, on the other hand, employees' claim to $5.00 per hour is not waivable, then Snyder's account is committed to holding that failing to benefit needy workers at all is better than benefiting them at a level that is (significantly) greater than zero but less than the morally required amount – even if workers themselves would strongly prefer and like to choose the latter over the former. This seems implausible, as well.

CONCLUSION

It is morally wrong to violate a person's rights. When it comes to using physical coercion to get sweatshop workers into a factory, all reasonable people in the sweatshop debate are on the same side. It is morally wrong and unethical to buy products made with coerced slave labor. It is also very rare. In the vast majority of sweatshops, workers are not physically coerced into working – they choose to. Most of this book has argued that the choice by the workers has important consequentialist implications, but their choice also has moral significance. Respecting a

---

[22] Actually, Snyder does not quite hold that it is "sufficient." Several other conditions must be met for the employer to have this duty, but as they do not affect the present argument, these need not concern us here.

worker's autonomy means respecting their choice to waive one of their rights when they deem it in their best interest. A person's right to their own body means a firm cannot demand that they work for the firm. But a person can waive a portion of their rights in order to work for a firm when the firm makes them an offer they deem in their best interest. *Negative rights* are rights protecting individuals from having things done to them. Everyone in the sweatshop debate agrees that workers have negative rights and that they can waive them when it is in their best interest.

Some scholars have argued that by interacting with sweatshop workers, firms (or consumers) acquire new positive duties that sweatshop workers have a right to. I have argued that if sweatshop workers start with no positive rights and acquire positive rights only by interacting with a firm, it would seem to be better if a firm benefited a worker a little bit, but less than what their positive right entitled them to, rather than not at all. Furthermore, even if a positive right exists, the worker may waive it, just as a negative right. Thus, firms are not wrongfully exploiting workers, so it seems ethical to buy products of sweatshop labor.

Yet people often feel "dirty" because they benefit from sweatshop labor, but they do not feel dirty because of the existence of Third World poverty. Part of the reason is that we do not directly benefit from the labor of the poor subsistence farmer. Another part of the reason is cognitive. As Matt Zwolinski put it, "Neglect might feel less wrong to us, because we are not cognizant of the value we are neglecting."[23]

But in his rendering, and mine, the fact that we benefit from sweatshop labor and are more cognizant of workers' plight does not change anything. As Zwolinski states:

If the persons we neglect are ... just as valuable as those with whom we are engaged, then it is hard to see how neglect could actually be less wrong. Similarly, if those we neglect are indeed as valuable as those with whom we are engaged, then it is also not clear how we come to acquire new obligations to persons just by virtue of being engaged with them. The value of the persons is the same whether we are engaged with them or not, and if the value is the same, so too should be our call to respect that value.[24]

---

[23] Zwolinski, "Sweatshops, Choice, and Exploitation," 710.
[24] Ibid.

Whether neglect of the plight of the poor is morally wrong is beyond the focus of this book. For my purposes, it is enough to argue that there is nothing special about sweatshop workers that entitles them to more than any other similarly poor person. In fact, the moral theories that put more weight on the welfare of the least-advantaged people should be much more concerned about the rest of the poor in the Third World because this book has shown that sweatshop workers are better off than most of them.[25]

The fact that sweatshops are these workers' best available option and that it is ethical to buy their products is not the end of the story. Even if the workers do not have a moral right to anything more from people, it does not mean that we do not wish they could obtain a higher standard of living. With that in mind, for the next three chapters, let us explore how sweatshops have been eliminated in countries that are wealthy today, and what good activists might be able to do to help current sweatshop workers.

[25] John Rawls, *A Theory of Justice* (Cambridge, MA: Harvard University Press, 1971).

8

A History of Sweatshops, 1780–2010

> Whenever I raise the point that it is immoral to shut us up in a close (sic) room twelve hours a day in the most monotonous and tedious of employment, I am told that we have come to the mills voluntarily and we can leave when we will. Voluntarily! ... The whip which brings us to Lowell is necessity. We must have money; a father's debts are to be paid, an aged mother to be supported, a brother's ambition to be aided and so the factories are supplied. Is this to act from free will? Is this freedom? To my mind it is slavery.[1]

These were the words, in 1845, of Sarah Bagley, who worked in Lowell, Massachusetts, and became the vice president of the Lowell Union of Associationists, a utopian reform organization. But they could easily be the words of an anti-sweatshop activist describing Third World sweatshops today.

Sweatshops are not new. They first appeared in Great Britain in the late eighteenth century and persisted there until the early twentieth century. In the United States, the first textile sweatshops appeared in the early nineteenth century in Rhode Island and Massachusetts. In fact, they flourished in the cities where I grew up and went to college. Lowell, Massachusetts and Lawrence, Massachusetts dominated the textile industry in the nineteenth century, and Haverhill, Massachusetts, my hometown, still has the nickname "the shoe city," which it earned in the nineteenth and early twentieth centuries because of all the shoe factories located there. Virtually every wealthy country in the world had sweatshops at one point in their past. Sweatshops are an important stage in the process of economic development. As Jeffery Sachs, an economist

---

[1] Quoted in Lowell Mills Museum, Lowell National Historical Park, Lowell, MA.

and director of the Earth Institute at Columbia University, put it, "Sweatshops are the first rung on the ladder out of extreme poverty."[2] Let us examine what that rung was like in countries that are wealthy today.

SWEATSHOPS IN NINETEENTH CENTURY GREAT BRITAIN AND THE UNITED STATES

Working conditions have been harsh and standards of living low throughout most of human history. Farmers worked long hours for near-subsistence returns for much of recent human history. There is no doubt that chattel slavery imposed horrid working conditions and standards of living on innumerable people throughout history. But it was not until the industrial revolution that something resembling modern-day sweatshops emerged.

Prior to the industrial revolution, textile production was decentralized to the homes of many rural families or artisans, and output was limited to what could be produced on the spinning wheel and hand loom. In 1833, the invention of the flying shuttle increased the demand for yarn by boosting the production of each weaver. Yarn spinning was mechanized in 1767 with the invention of the spinning jenny, and water power was harnessed shortly thereafter. With these inventions, and later steam power, large-scale textile factories that are similar to today's sweatshops emerged.

The conditions in these early sweatshops were worse than those in many Third World sweatshops today. In some factories, workers toiled for sixteen hours a day, six days per week. Attendance at traditional festival days was curtailed because factories would fine workers for absences. The working conditions were unhealthy and dangerous. Dust from textile fibers was inhaled from poorly ventilated rooms, and workers were maimed by fast-moving machinery.[3] Child labor was common. Factories employed orphan children from London and other

---

[2] Jeffrey Sachs, *The End of Poverty: Economic Possibilities for Our Time* (New York: Penguin Press, 2005), 11.

[3] Peter Stearns, *The Industrial Revolution in World History*, 3rd ed. (Boulder: Westview Press, 2007), 35.

major cities in exchange for providing them room and board.[4] As historian Peter Sterns summarized it, "Extensive use of child and female labor was not in itself novel – families had always depended on work by all members to survive – but use of children and young women specifically because of the low wages they could be pressed to accept reflected the pressures of early industrial life and unquestionably constrained the nascent working class in the factories."[5]

It was not just the work in the factories that was dangerous. The cities themselves were unhealthy. Their swelling population and poor sanitation led to the spread of disease. Housing was cramped, poorly constructed, and sometimes expensive. On many margins, the quality of life in cities was lower than in the country. But workers flocked to the mills. The proportion of people in Great Britain living in cities with more than 5,000 people rose from 21 percent in 1750 to 28 percent in 1800 and then ballooned to 45 percent by 1850.[6] Meanwhile, the share of the labor force working in agriculture shrank from 35 percent in 1801 to 22 percent in 1851.[7] Why did people move to the cities in such numbers? It was partly due to involuntary enclosure of agricultural lands, but also, much as today's Third World sweatshop workers, they were attracted by the opportunity to earn higher wages than they could elsewhere. In fact, economist Ludwig Von Mises defended the factory system of the industrial revolution in much the same manner as I have defended modern sweatshops, writing, "The factory owners did not have the power to compel anybody to take a factory job. They could only hire people who were ready to work for the wages offered to them. Low as these wage rates were, they were nonetheless more

---

[4] An important distinction within child labor during Britain's industrial revolution is often overlooked. There were "free-labour" children who lived with their families and freely chose to work, and there were "apprentice children" who were orphans and under the direct control of government officials. Many of the worst accounts of child labor during this time describe factories employing apprentice children who were forced to work by the authority of the state. The first reform laws were targeted at the abuses of apprentice children who did not have normal market mechanisms protecting them. See Lawrence Reed, "Child Labor and the British Industrial Revolution," *The Freeman* 41, No. 8 (1991). http://www.fee.org/the_freeman/detail/child-labor-and-the-british-industrial-revolution/#axzz2bCgbEqL4

[5] Stearns, *The Industrial Revolution*, 34.

[6] Joel Mokyr, *The Enlightened Economy: An Economic History of Britain, 1700–1850* (New Haven: Yale University Press, 2009), 456.

[7] Mokyr, *The Enlightened Economy*, 476.

than these paupers could earn in any other field open to them."[8] He continued:

It is a distortion of facts to say that the factories carried off the housewives from the nurseries and the kitchens and the children from their play. These women had nothing to cook with and to feed their children. These children were destitute and starving. Their only refuge was the factory. It saved them, in the strict sense of the term, from death by starvation.[9]

Mises's argument is supported by historical evidence. Economist Joel Mokyr reports that workers earned a wage premium of 15–30 percent by working in the factories compared with other alternatives.[10] The transformation of Great Britain during this time was dramatic. As economist and historian Deirdre McCloskey describes it,

In the 80 years or so after 1780 the population of Britain nearly tripled, the towns of Liverpool and Manchester became gigantic cities, the average income of the population more than doubled, the share of farming fell from just under half to just under one-fifth of the nation's output, and the making of textiles and iron moved into steam-driven factories.[11]

The increased income translated into meaningful improvements in the standard of living. McCloskey reports that "the amounts of bread, beer, trousers, shoes, trips to London, warmth in winter, and protection against conquest increased from 11 (pounds) per head in 1780 to 28 in 1860. ... Because he produced two-and-a-half times more than his great-grandfather produced in 1780, the average person in 1860 could buy two-and-a-half times more goods and services."[12] Similarly, Peter Lindert and Jeffery Williamson find impressive gains in the standard of living between 1781 and 1851. They find that farm labor's standard of living went up more than 60 percent, blue collar workers' standard increased more than 86 percent, and overall workers' standard increased more than 140 percent. Along with this increase in the standard of living came a decrease in the share of women and children working beginning

---

[8] Mises, *Human Action* (Auburn, NY: Ludwig Von Mises Institute, 1998), 615.
[9] Ibid.
[10] Mokyr, *The Enlightened Economy*, 457.
[11] Deirdre McCloskey, "The Industrial Revolution 1780–1860: A Survey," in *The Economics of the Industrial Revolution*, ed. Joel Mokyr (New Jersey: Rowman and Allanheld, 1985), 53.
[12] McCloskey, "The Industrial Revolution 1780–1860: A Survey," 56.

sometime between 1815 and 1820. As Lindert and Williamson summarize, "The hardships faced by workers at the end of the Industrial Revolution cannot have been nearly as great as those of their grandparents."[13]

By 1851, Great Britain's per capita income stood at $2,362.00. This was 65 percent higher than that in Germany and 30 percent higher than that in the United States.[14] Some historians debate whether the industrial revolution improved the standard of living much before 1820. An analysis is complicated by an expensive foreign war and other unfavorable external circumstances. At a minimum, they agree that the early industrial revolution prevented the standard of living from falling when facing these circumstances plus an enormous increase in the population, which traditionally would have been expected to drag down standards of living. But there is little doubt that there was a meaningful improvement in people's living standards during the first seventy years of the industrial revolution. All but the most willfully blind can recognize that living standards improved greatly for the generations born within the century following 1850.

The industrial revolution began in Great Britain, but the United States was one of the earlier places to which it was exported. When textile production was mechanized in Great Britain, all of the technology had to be created, and new capital had to be accumulated that could embody that technology. The United States was in a position more like many Third World countries today. It could import technology and capital from abroad to jump-start its industrial revolution. The British were extremely secretive and protective of their technology. But eventually Samuel Slater, who had worked his way up from apprentice to overseer in a British factory, immigrated to America with the plans for an Arkwright water frame memorized. In 1790, he set up the first cotton-spinning mill in the United States in Rhode Island. At first, textile factories in the United States were limited to carding and spinning. Then Francis Cabot Lowell introduced a workable power loom, and all stages of textile production were integrated into a single factory.

---

[13] Peter Lindert and Jeffrey Williamson, "English Workers' Living Standards during the Industrial Revolution: A New Look," in *The Economics of the Industrial Revolution*, ed. Joel Mokyr (New Jersey: Rowman and Allanheld, 1985).

[14] Mokyr, *The Enlightened Economy*, 476.

He and his associates opened a factory in Waltham, Massachusetts, in 1814 and went on to found factories in Lowell, Lawrence, and throughout New England.

Later, particularly in the latter half of the nineteenth century and on, the United States contributed many of its own technological breakthroughs, but for much of the nineteenth century it remained dependent on foreign technological advances. At first, U.S. businesses imitated technology mostly from Britain and France; later, in industries such as chemicals, they imitated the Germans and Swedish.[15] The United States also embraced the investment of foreign capital. Peter Stearns reports that "the United States also relied unusually heavily on foreign capital. The nation was rich in resources but lacked the funds to develop them as rapidly as industrialization required. Huge investments from Europe, in particular Great Britain, fueled U.S. industry throughout the nineteenth century."[16]

This infusion of foreign capital and technology allowed the United States to proceed through its industrial revolution more rapidly than Great Britain. In 1820, before the United States had started its industrial revolution, its per capita income was just more than $2,000.00 – the approximate British income level in 1700. But by 1903, roughly seventy-five years into its industrial revolution, the United States had caught up to Britain's per capita income.[17]

The infusion of foreign capital and technology did not allow the United States to skip the stage of sweatshop development, however. Early textile factories were similar to those in Great Britain at that time, and the Third World today. Hours were long. In 1845, more than 2,000 Lowell textile workers unsuccessfully petitioned the state legislature for a ten-hour work day. Their petition described some of their working conditions:

We the undersigned peaceable, industrious and hard working men and women of Lowell, in view of our condition – the evils already come upon us, by toiling from 13 to 14 hours per day, confined in unhealthy apartments, exposed to

---

[15] Stearns, *The Industrial Revolution*, 62.

[16] Stearns, *The Industrial Revolution*, 66.

[17] Income figures are updated for inflation to 2010 U.S. dollars from Maddison's income data, which was in constant 1990 International Keary-Khamis dollars. Angus Maddison, retrieved from http://www.ggdc.net/maddison/test/.

poisonous contagion of air, vegetable, animal and mineral properties, debarred from proper physical exercise, mental discipline, and mastication cruelly limited, and thereby hastening us on through pain disease and privation, down to a premature grave, pray the legislature to institute a ten hour working day in all of the factories of the state.[18]

I visited the National Historic Park at the Lowell Mills while writing this chapter. The descriptions of the work environment in the museum there could be a description of many of the Third World sweatshops today:

Weave rooms were hazardous work environments. Life threatening accidents and long term health disabilities were common by products of employment in the textile mills. Cotton dust caused lung and respiratory diseases. The noise was deafening and impaired hearing. The lighting was poor, the hours long, the work tedious, and the machinery and belting dangerous.

In the weave room, both heat and humidity are kept high to prevent the yarn from breaking. Workers, who were paid by the piece, were often willing to endure the humidity because it increased both productivity and their pay checks. Nevertheless, work in this environment was eventually debilitating.

Compared to agricultural life, a worker's day was highly regimented and hectic. As one woman described it in a trade newspaper in 1841, "I object to the constant hurry of everything. We cannot have time to eat, drink, or sleep; we have only thirty minutes, or at most three quarters of an hour, allowed us, to go from our work, partake of our food, and return to the noisy clatter of machinery."[19]

But despite these conditions, workers flocked to the mills. At first, in the cities north of Boston it was mainly rural women and girls who left the farm to populate the early textile mills.[20] During the 1830s in Lowell, a woman could earn $12.00–$14.00 a month, and after paying $5.00 for room and board in a company boarding house would have the rest left over for clothing, leisure, and savings. It was not uncommon for women to return home to the farm after a year with $25.00–$50.00 in a bank account. This is far more money than they could have earned

---

[18] Published in *Voice of Industry*, January 15, 1845.

[19] *The Lowell Offering*, 1841.

[20] The factory system in these cities was known as the "Waltham System." South of Boston, factories employed the "Rhode Island System," which tended to hire entire families.

on the farm and often more disposable cash than their fathers had.[21] There was another benefit for the women, as well. For many it was the first time they had any independence from their fathers. For the first time, they earned their own money, lived on their own, and could choose their leisure activities without male interference.[22] The mill cities availed the young women with many amenities, from libraries to public lectures to wider consumer goods options than they had had in their rural lives. The story of a young female factory worker in the early nineteenth-century United States is not unlike situations described now in China in which young rural women move to the factories for both better pay and greater independence despite tough working conditions.

Eventually, as women demanded greater pay and more competitors in other regions entered the textile market, immigrants came to be the main textile workers in the United States. Still, much as Great Britain, living standards improved over time. In 1820, before the industrial revolution, per capita income in the United States stood at just over $2,000.00. By 1850, it had grown by 50 percent to more than $3,000.00, and then it doubled again by 1900 to more than $6,600.00.[23] Along with the rise in incomes came improvements in working conditions and greater consumption. By 1900, ten-hour work days were becoming more common, and weekends were beginning to include Saturdays or at least Saturday afternoons off.[24] New forms of leisure also expanded and were related to advances in industry:

Much of the new leisure also depended on industrial technology, from the tram lines that took the urban masses to large concrete and metal stadiums, to the vulcanized rubber balls that were mass-produced from the 1840s onward. Clearly a revolution in leisure was underway, but it came a bit later than the industrial revolution itself. ... By the late nineteenth century, however, consumerism could be more widely indulged throughout the West. New products

---

[21] National Park Service, "Lowell: The Story of an Industrial City," *Official National Park Handbook*, Handbook 140, Division of Publications National Park Service, U.S. Department of the Interior (Washington, DC, 1992), 40.

[22] See Jeff Levinson, *Mill Girls of Lowell*, ed. J. Levinson (Boston: History Compass, 2007).

[23] Income figures are updated for inflation to 2010 U.S. dollars from Maddison's income data, which was in constant 1990 International Keary-Khamis dollars.

[24] Stearns, *The Industrial Revolution*, 175–176.

like bicycles – an 1880s fad – and the automobile represented more expensive consumer items than had ever before been sold widely.[25]

In both Great Britain and the United States from 1900 onward, incomes continued to rise, hours were reduced, and working conditions improved. By midway through the twentieth century, anything that could be mean-ingfully labeled a sweatshop for textile or apparel production ceased to operate on any widespread basis. In Great Britain, depending on when one dates the start of the industrial revolution and how stringent one requires wage and working-condition standards to be for a factory to be a sweatshop, the process of development involving sweatshops lasted from 130 to 160 years. In the United States, the process was faster, taking around 100 years. When we look at countries that have developed more recently, we see an even faster process of development.

POST–WORLD WAR II EAST ASIAN SWEATSHOP DEVELOPMENT SUCCESSES

If when you think about South Korea, Taiwan, Hong Kong, or Singapore you think of a wealthy First World country, you are right; they are. South Korea and Taiwan have per capita income levels on par with the 1990s United States, and Hong Kong and Singapore are roughly on par with current U.S. income levels. But that was not always the case. Just sixty years ago, Hong Kong and Singapore had per capita income levels around $3,700.00, and Taiwan and South Korea's levels were around $1,500.00 per capita. At that time, U.S. income levels were around $16,000.00 per capita.[26] In 1950, these four East Asian countries were at roughly pre–industrial revolution income levels, and like the United States and Great Britain more than a century earlier, they went through a sweatshop stage of economic development. But in these East Asian countries the process of moving from sweatshops to a wealthy First World nation took less than two generations rather than the more than 100 years in Great Britain and the United States.

Although the mix of industries involved in the development of each of these economies differed, a commonality ran through them. All of

---

[25] Stearns, *The Industrial Revolution*, 176.

[26] Income figures are updated for inflation to 2010 U.S. dollars from Maddison's income data, which was in constant 1990 International Keary-Khamis dollars.

these countries took advantage of their relatively cheap labor to produce textiles and often inexpensive consumer plastics for export. These
factories often had long hours and poor working conditions, much the
same as Third World sweatshops today. Peter Stearns briefly summarizes some of the growth in these countries:

> Taiwanese manufacturing sold widely around the world. Inexpensive con-
> sumer items, including plastic products and textiles, became a Taiwanese
> hallmark. ... Korea was competing successfully in cheap consumer goods,
> like plastics ... the same held true in textiles. ... Oil refineries and textiles
> and electronics factories joined shipbuilding as major sectors [in Singapore]....
> Export production in industry, particularly in textiles, combined high-speed
> technology with low wages and long hours for the labor force to yield highly
> competitive results.[27]

The textile exports from these countries eliminated almost one-third
of textile jobs in wealthier and more expensive Japan.[28] In fact, Japan
focused on high-tech production and came to rely on these countries
for less-expensive factory goods that were once key exports when
Japan had its industrial surge.

Of course, cheap sweatshop production was not the only industry in
these countries, but it was an important part of their recipe for development: "Although textiles and clothing formed 39 percent of Hong
Kong's exports by the 1980s, other sectors, including heavy industry,
had developed impressively as well. As in other Pacific Rim industrial
nations, a large and prosperous middle class developed."[29] Eventually,
as incomes rose, the sweatshops began to disappear in these countries,
just as they did in the United States. These nations began shifting to
higher-productivity sectors, and their textile factories saw stiffer competition from other nations with lower standards of living. The sweatshops moved from these East Asian tigers to many of the places where
we see them today. Sweatshops were a necessary stage in their process
of development but one that they moved beyond, and did so more
quickly than Great Britain and the United States.

---

[27] Stearns, *The Industrial Revolution*, 223, 225.
[28] Stearns, *The Industrial Revolution*, 223.
[29] Stearns, *The Industrial Revolution*, 226.

WHAT ROLE DO NATIONAL LABOR LAWS PLAY?

Sweatshops are eliminated mainly through the process of industrialization that raises a country's income. The increased income comes from increased worker productivity. That raises the upper bound of compensation. The increased productivity is not just in one firm but in many firms and industries, and thus workers' next best alternatives improve, raising the lower bound of compensation. Thus, as the economy grows, the competitive process pushes wages up. Because health, safety, leisure, and so forth are normal goods, workers demand more of their compensation on these margins as their total compensation increases. The result is the eventual disappearance of sweatshops. An obvious point that critics should raise concerns the adoption of labor laws. Didn't the minimum wages, laws against child labor, maximum work-hour laws, and health and safety standards laws play a role in eliminating sweatshops? If they did historically in the United States and Great Britain, shouldn't other developing countries adopt them now?

The short answer is that the laws played very little role in ending sweatshop conditions. For the most part, the laws were adopted once the United States had already reached a level of development that had mostly eliminated the conditions the laws made illegal. As explained in Chapter 7, Great Britain's first restrictions on child labor applied only to children under nine years old, and Massachusetts's child labor law, the first in the United States, only limited the workday to ten hours for children under twelve. The United States did not pass meaningful national legislation against child labor until 1938, when its per capita income was more than $10,200.00 (in 2010 dollars). Economist Price Fishback explains the process that led to the adoption of the child labor laws:

Child labor laws appear to exemplify existing social trends coinciding with or preceding legislation. Between 1880 and 1920, the labor market participation rates of children fell nearly sixfold, while a well-organized social movement pressured state legislatures to enact limits on child employment. Studies of this period suggest that relatively little of the decline in child participation rates can be attributed to the introduction of child labor legislation. ... As their demand for child labor fell, the employers who had already eliminated it reduced their opposition to child labor laws. In fact, they may have actively supported the legislation to force recalcitrant employers to follow in their footsteps.[30]

The process of limiting working hours for women was similar: "State laws limiting the number of working hours for women may also have passed after many employers had substantially reduced hours for women. Recent studies have found that the laws had relatively little effect. . . . The legislation acted mainly to limit hours for a small number of women who had not yet succeeded in negotiating reduction in hours."[31]

Similarly, as explained in Chapter 3, the first federal U.S. minimum wage was not introduced until 1938, and it set the minimum at 25 cents per hour – when average productivity was already 62.7 cents. The first state minimum wage law was not passed until 1912 in Massachusetts, and it applied only to women and children. Other national labor legislation did not come until the United States was even more developed. Maximum work-hour legislation was introduced in 1940, occupational health and safety was not passed until 1970, and maternity leave was not introduced until 1993.

The same pattern is true of workplace safety regulation. Fishback finds that "most [safety] regulations appear to have codified existing practices in the relevant industry."[32] When safety laws were passed that exceeded industry standards, they often were not enforced. Potentially dangerous mines were inspected, at most, only once or twice a year, and factory inspections were even more limited: "Spending on factory inspection may have been less effective than spending on mine inspection. The number of factories per inspector was huge, making it impossible for inspectors to visit all workplaces within a year."[33] The anti-sweatshop movement often points to the famous 1911 Triangle Shirtwaist Factory fire as evidence of the need for regulation. But Fishback finds that the deaths in that fire "could be attributed in part to violations of building and factory codes that had gone unpunished. Soon after New York State tightened the laws, however, New York

---

[30] Price Fishback, *Government and the American Economy: A New History* (Chicago: University of Chicago Press, 2007), 307–308.
[31] Fishback, "The Progressive Era," 308.
[32] Fishback, "The Progressive Era," 310–311.
[33] Fishback, "The Progressive Era," 311.

newspapers were still describing the inadequacies of enforcement, and statistical studies show no effect of state factory inspection budgets on accident rates."[34] In short, when laws mandated greater safety than industry practice, they were often ignored, much as they are in Third World sweatshops today. Safety improved instead in response to economic growth.

This is not to say that none of these laws had any effect. There are always occasional firms that lag behind or some low-skilled workers who are affected. As Chapters 3 and 5 explain, unemployment for the least skilled is the main effect of these types of laws. The point is that the United States did not adopt these labor laws until most workers' compensation and productivity already exceeded what the law mandates.[35] Thus, the United States did not experience major disruptions in its process of development because of the laws. When the laws did set a standard above the norm, such as the first minimum wage in Puerto Rico, the result was a disaster.

All too often people see the strict labor laws in the United States and assume that they must be the cause of the good standards rather than the codification of what had already happened. Ludwig Von Mises explained, "The nineteenth century's labor legislation by and large achieved nothing more than to provide a legal ratification for changes which the interplay of market factors had brought about previously."[36] If the United States had today's labor laws in the mid-nineteenth century, the result would have been massive unemployment and a halt to the development process. An excellent study by economists Joshua Hall and Peter Leeson, amusingly titled "Good for the Goose, Bad for the Gander," makes this point for sweatshop countries today.[37]

---

[34] Ibid.

[35] Matthias Busse shows that higher per capita income, increased openness to trade, and enhanced human capital are all positively associated with the level of core labor standards a country adopts, and that income is the most important factor in explaining differences in forced and child labor as well as unionization rights. See Busse, "On the Determinants of Core Labor Standards: The Case of Developing Countries," *Economics Letters* 83, No. 2 (May 2004), 211–217.

[36] Mises, *Human Action*, 612.

[37] Joshua Hall and Peter Leeson, "Good for the Goose, Bad for the Gander: International Labor Standards and Comparative Development," *Journal of Labor Research* 28, No. 4 (September 2007), 658–676. Incidentally, although their title is amusing, it would be more accurate, if less pithy, if it were "Mostly Indifferent for the Goose: Bad for the Gander."

Table 8.1 *U.S. Income and Labor Standards Compared
to Sweatshop Countries*

Labor Standard	Date of U.S. Adoption	U.S. GDP/Capita Introduced	No. of Years Until Avg. Sweatshop Country Reaches U.S. Income Level at Time of Adoption
Collective bargaining	1935	$9,123.00	29
Child labor	1938	$10,223.00	35
Minimum wage	1938	$10,223.00	35
Occup. safety & health	1970	$25,081.00	80
Unemploment insurance	1935	$9,123.00	29
Equality of opportunity	1964	$21,314.00	72
Working time	1940	$11,698.00	42
Maternity leave	1993	$39,176.00	102

Source: Hall and Leeson 2007.

If they were to adopt and enforce U.S.-style labor laws, it would cut their process of development short. Hall and Leeson document the level of development the United States had achieved when it adopted each of its major labor laws and compare it to the level of development in countries that use sweatshops intensively today.[38] They calculated the average income in each of the sweatshop countries and then extrapolate from their recent rates of economic growth how many years it will take them to reach the level of development the United States had achieved when it adopted each of its major labor standards. Table 8.1 summarizes the main labor standards in the United States, when these standards were adopted, the U.S. average income at the time of adoption, and how many years Hall and Leeson project the average sweatshop country is from reaching that income level.[39]

---

[38] Their list of sweatshop-intensive countries included Bangladesh, Brazil, China, Costa Rica, Dominican Republic, El Salvador, Haiti, Honduras, India, Indonesia, Nicaragua, Peru, and Vietnam.

[39] U.S. income figures are updated for inflation to 2010 U.S. dollars from Maddison's income data, which was in constant 1990 International Keary-Khamis dollars.

Countries where sweatshops locate have per capita incomes far below those the United States had when it adopted the type of labor standards many people want Third World countries to enforce today. Given their recent rates of economic growth, most of these countries are many years away from reaching a level of development at which adopting such standards would not risk undermining the development process. Although that message may seem depressing, it need not be. Although the process of growth that ended sweatshops in Great Britain and the United States took more than 100 years, and many of the current sweatshop countries are growing slowly today, the process need not take that long anymore, as a quick look at some East Asian success stories revealed.

CONCLUSION

Anti-sweatshop activist Dan Viederman claims that "there are centuries of proof that jobs that are created without respect to ethical or legal standards do not make workers or societies more prosperous. December's factory fire in Bangladesh, where 20 people died, proves the point dramatically."[40] Of course, that fire no more proves that jobs in sweatshops do not make societies more prosperous than a house fire proves that housing does not generally provide superior shelter to dwelling in caves. More importantly, the brief review of the history of sweatshops in this chapter shows how wrong he is about jobs created without respect to ethical and legal standards. Factories with poor working conditions existed long before substantial legal standards, these jobs made these countries more prosperous, and that prosperity, rather than legal standards, led to improved wages and working conditions. This lesson is vitally important to understand if activists want to improve the lives of sweatshop workers today. We need to understand how the process of development works, the role sweatshops play in that process, and what commonality the East Asian tigers, the United States, and Great Britain had that allowed them to develop whereas many nations have remained poor.

---

[40] Dan Viederman, "Any Job Is a Good Job? Think Again," *Huffington Post*, February 18, 2011.

9

The Process of Economic Development

The process of economic development has been the greatest poverty cure in human history. Over the past 200 years, this process has eradicated countless sweatshops and replaced them with better jobs. Understanding this process is crucial for those who want to improve the lives of today's sweatshop workers.

People living in First World countries today often seem to forget that their living standards are the exception, not the norm, in our history. Most of man's existence has been mired in poverty with prospects for a short life and famine a constant threat. Great Britain and the United States were among the first countries to break out of that dismal cycle. Fortunately, many other countries have joined them today.

To achieve and maintain a high standard of living, a country's workers need to have a high level of productivity. In other words, they need to get a lot of valuable output for every hour they work. The proximate causes of high productivity are physical capital, human capital, and technology. Sweatshops play a role in increasing all three of these.

Understanding human capital's role in development is the most straightforward. When workers have greater skills, they are able to get more output out of a given level of inputs. These greater skills can come from formal education, but they can also come from experience and on-the-job training. On-the-job learning can be important for developing greater human capital, particularly in low-skilled occupations. Think of the opportunities facing many Third World workers. For many, learning how to stitch quickly can be more valuable than learning the higher-level math or even basic English that they might get in formal education. In any event, both formal education and on-the-job training are ways to build human capital. Which builds more human capital depends on the endowment of the particular person and the opportunities available to them at the time.

Physical capital is vitally important to having a high standard of living. The most brilliant man in the world would quickly starve if he did not have any tools to work with. But capital goods, such as tools, machinery, factories, buildings, and the computer I typed this chapter on all must be created. Capital is created when people forgo some current consumption to use scarce resources to create the capital that will later produce even more consumption goods for them. Capital comes from savings. This is one reason the industrial revolution took so long to produce higher standards of living in Great Britain. Current consumption had to be forgone and capital slowly accumulated. As productivity and profits rose, there was a greater ability to save and create even more capital. As Peter Stearns put it, "Rising output boosted industrial profits, which provided additional capital for still further changes, and began to permit some definite if modest improvements in the standard of living of most workers."[1] Ludwig Von Mises summarizes the crucial role prior capital accumulation plays in our standard of living, writing, "The heritage of the past embodied in our supply of capital goods is our wealth and the foremost means of further advancement in well-being."[2]

The East Asian success stories had a distinct advantage over Great Britain when they developed. Their capital formation could happen much faster because they could draw on savings from wealthy countries in addition to their own savings. When foreign firms made investments in those countries, they created many of the buildings and machines that the citizens of Hong Kong, Singapore, Taiwan, and South Korea would work with. The same is true in poor countries today. When multinational companies open up sweatshops in Third World countries, they are using the savings in First World countries to create capital in Third World countries. Over time, the accumulation of capital in these countries leads to increased productivity and higher standards of living.

---

[1] Peter Stearns, *The Industrial Revolution in World History*, 3rd ed. (Boulder: Westview Press, 2007), 37.

[2] Ludwig Von Mises, *Human Action* (Auburn, NY: Ludwig Von Mises Institute, 1998), 510.

Although capital accumulation is crucial for economic development, it alone cannot explain high standards of living. A larger and
larger capital stock will take larger and larger amounts of savings just
to maintain it. To maximize living standards, you also have to get more
production out of any given amount of capital. When it comes to the
industrial revolution, McCloskey summarizes the point nicely:

> Had the machines and men of 1860 embodied the same knowledge of how to
> spin cotton or move cargo that they had in 1780, the larger number of spindles
> and ships would have barely offset the fixity of land.... The larger quantities of
> capital did make some difference. ... But the larger part of the difference
> between this dismal possibility and the 28 pounds per head actually achieved
> by 1860 was attributable to better technology.[3]

Better technology allows people to obtain more output from both their
labor and capital inputs. In Great Britain, much of this technology
needed to be invented for capital goods to embody it. But as we saw
earlier, when the United States began to industrialize, it copied much
of the technology that was already created in Great Britain.
Furthermore, the United States benefited from foreign investment
that brought new technologies with it. The same process is happening
in Third World countries today.

Sweatshops do not just provide a better job than the really lousy
other options in these countries. Sweatshops themselves are part of the
very process of development that will lead to their own elimination.[4]
When foreigners make investments in Third World sweatshops, they
bring in capital and new technologies as well as give workers an
opportunity to build human capital. All three of these things contribute
to making workers more productive, which ultimately raises their
wages and leads to improved jobs.

Although accumulating capital, improving technology, and creating
a more skilled work force are necessary for achieving a high standard
of living, they are not sufficient. It is not simply "capital" that needs to

---

[3] Deirdre McCloskey, "The Industrial Revolution 1780–1860: A Survey," in *The
Economics of the Industrial Revolution*, ed. Joel Mokyr (New Jersey: Rowman and
Allanheld, 1985), 57.

[4] For more on the process of development, including several recent case studies of some
of the biggest successes and failures in development, see Benjamin Powell, *Making
Poor Nations Rich: Entrepreneurship and the Process of Development*, ed. B. Powell
(Palo Alto, CA: Stanford University Press, 2008).

be accumulated. Capital is heterogeneous, that is, an office building and a sewing machine are both capital, but they serve different purposes, so the right capital needs to be accumulated.[5] The right capital is the capital that best complements the existing capital and labor to produce the greatest value for society in the ultimate production of consumer goods. To find out what capital is best, we need the market's competitive process to operate.

Prices are conveyers of information about relative scarcity. Prices of consumer goods indicate how much value people place on different items. Entrepreneurs then bid on inputs, including capital goods, to make those consumer goods. The ability to buy all the necessary inputs and still sell the consumer goods for a profit is a signal that entrepreneurs have created value for society by transforming valuable inputs into a more valuable output. Losses are a signal that entrepreneurs are destroying value by taking scarce resources that could have been used to produce something else and turning those resources into less-valuable final consumer goods. The market's profit and loss system provides the feedback on which businesses and industries should expand and which contract.

Capital goods get their value from the final consumer goods they create. But any given capital good can play a role in producing more than one consumer good. Thus, the alternative uses of the capital good need to be weighed against each other. This is what happens when entrepreneurs bid against each other for capital goods. Each entrepreneur is assessing how much value he expects he can create by using the capital good, and that informs him of how much he is willing to bid for it. Those entrepreneurs who think they can create the greatest value outbid those who do not think they can create as much. This process helps allocate a given capital stock most efficiently. The array of capital goods prices also tells us how valuable different capital goods are. These prices signal other entrepreneurs to create more of the most valuable capital and enable them to profit by doing it.

---

[5] For more on the important implications of capital heterogeneity for economic theory, see Benjamin Powell "Some Implications of Capital Heterogeneity," *Handbook on Contemporary Austrian Economics*, ed. Peter Boettke (Cheltenham, UK: Edward Elgar, 2010).

Market prices play the key role in transmitting the relevant information necessary for growth to occur. First, they signal consumers' desires for consumption goods. Then, they signal the relative scarcity of capital goods in alternative uses through the bidding of entrepreneurs. Finally, the capital goods prices signal what new capital should be created. Prices convey the information, and because entrepreneurs have property rights in their profits and losses, they have the right incentive to only use capital goods where they can create the greatest value.

Absent this competitive process, no one knows which capital should be created to best promote economic growth. There is simply no way to harness the subjective expectations and valuations of all of the market participants without giving them the autonomy to act on their own. There has been no shortage of failed attempts to simply stuff "capital" into poorer countries to help them develop. Foreign aid for investment in capital through the financing gap model was the World Bank's largest development program over the last sixty years, and it was a failure. One reason it failed is because it lacks the price system that harnesses economic calculation to determine what capital should be created.[6] Aid for investment or national economic planning that attempts to guide the structure of industry suffers from the economic calculation problem that – as economist Ludwig Von Mises correctly determined – socialist economies cannot solve.[7] Absent a market to decide which capital goods should be created and how they should be allocated, there is no relative scarcity indicator to indicate what capital should be created.

Although entrepreneurs are crucial for making the system work, they do not do so out of any conscious effort to promote efficiency or development. They are simply greedy profit seekers. Whenever the price system conveys the information that they can make a profit, they will seize the opportunity. That means when the price system conveys the wrong information, entrepreneurs could hinder development by making profits.

---

[6] Aid for investment and other aid programs also failed because they did not get the incentives right. On the role of incentives in these programs, see William Easterly, *The Elusive Quest for Growth* (Cambridge, MA: MIT Press, 2002).

[7] See Ludwig Von Mises, *Economic Calculation in the Socialist Commonwealth* (Auburn, AL: Ludwig Von Mises Institute, 1990).

Economist William Baumol pointed out that entrepreneurship can be productive, unproductive, or destructive.[8] The process of socially productive entrepreneurship is that previously described. Socially unproductive entrepreneurship occurs when an entrepreneur profits without on net creating or taking any value from society. Socially destructive entrepreneurship occurs when an entrepreneur profits by making society poorer, for example, when an entrepreneur successfully lobbies the government for a tariff barrier.

Because entrepreneurs are simply seeking profits and are largely indifferent to whether those profits are socially beneficial or not, it is crucial for economic development that the institutional environment promotes productive entrepreneurship while limiting opportunities for unproductive and destructive entrepreneurship as much as possible. That environment is one of strong private property rights and economic freedom.

ECONOMIC FREEDOM: THE ENVIRONMENT
FOR PRODUCTIVE ENTREPRENEURSHIP

To best promote development, market prices must accurately convey information about the relative scarcity of goods. This requires people to have strong property rights and the ability to freely exchange them on whatever terms they voluntarily agree on. Anything that impedes voluntary exchanges also impedes the price system's ability to convey the information necessary for economic calculation. Without private property, exchange is not possible. Inflation distorts the monetary system's ability to convey accurate prices. Taxes drive a wedge between people who would otherwise find gains from trade and thus their valuations do not impact prices. Regulations that prohibit trades or control prices distort the system. Economic freedom is harmed whenever governments interfere on these margins.

Although we understand intuitively what economic freedom entails, it is not easily objectively quantifiable. Economists began trying to measure economic freedom in the 1990s. The *Economic Freedom of the World* report, now coauthored by James Gwartney, Robert Lawson,

---

[8] William Baumol, "Entrepreneurship: Productive, Unproductive, and Destructive," *Journal of Political Economy* 98, No. 5 (1990), 893–921.

and Josh Hall, is the most widely used scholarly index that attempts to measure economic freedom across countries.[9] They measure economic freedom across five areas: the size of government; legal structure and property rights; freedom to trade internationally; sound money; and regulation of labor, credit, and business. An explosion of research using their index has occurred over the past fifteen years.[10]

The main finding in the literature is that economic freedom is beneficial for almost every measurable margin we care about in economic development. Economic freedom is associated with higher levels of per capita income, higher rates of economic growth, higher levels of entrepreneurial activity, higher rates of domestic investment, larger amounts of foreign investment, greater productivity of investment, longer life expectancies, better access to safe water, and lower infant mortality, among other things. Although more sophisticated empirical work showing the relationship between economic freedom and income has been done, Figure 9.1 presents the basic relationship. Figure 9.2

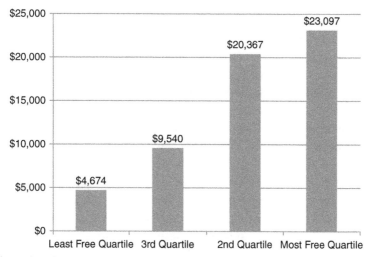

Figure 9.1 GDP per capita.

[9] James Gwartney, Robert Lawson, and Joshua Hall, *Economic Freedom of the World Annual Report* (Vancouver, BC, Canada: The Fraser Institute, 2011).

[10] For an earlier survey of this literature, see N. Berggren, "The Benefits of Economic Freedom," *The Independent Review* 8, No. 2 (Fall 2003), 193–211. The Fraser Institute also maintains a Web site with many of the published papers that use the index: http://www.freetheworld.com/papers.html.

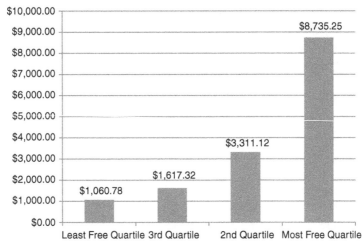

Figure 9.2 Income of the poorest 10 percent of the population.

illustrates that the gains in income associated with freedom do not just accrue to the wealthy but translate into increased income for the poorest members of society, as well.

Not only do levels of economic freedom matter, but changes in freedom matter, as well. Countries that improve in economic freedom, regardless of their initial level, tend to grow faster than other countries. An old economics joke serves as a good metaphor for understanding why. Two economists are walking down the sidewalk, and the junior economist says, "Look, there's a $100 bill lying on the sidewalk." The senior economist scoffs, "No. There can't be because it would already have been picked up." So the joke is not that funny, but it can serve a purpose here. In a normal economy, as profit opportunities pop up, entrepreneurs quickly seize them so that they are not left sitting there unexploited for others to take advantage of. Normal economic growth consists of the constant seizing of these opportunities as an economy chugs along. When economic freedom is suppressed, opportunities that should be profitably seized are not because laws or regulations prohibit it. It is as if a metal grate suspends people above the sidewalk so that they cannot reach down and grab the $100 bills. When economic freedom increases, it is like lowering the metal grate: all of a sudden, a whole bunch of big bills are within reach. When economic freedom increases, lots of profit opportunities suddenly become available.

Entrepreneurs seize them, and as a result growth takes off. A lot of research has shown that improvements in freedom matter as much as or more than the absolute levels for rapid growth.

The research on the effects of economic freedom is consistent with the narrative I have told about sweatshops and the process of development in this chapter. The industrial revolution began and flourished in Great Britain. During this time Great Britain was eliminating its mercantilist restrictions and respecting individual liberty and economic freedom. It had both a high level of economic freedom, and although it was not formally measured, economic freedom was clearly increasing. In her recent history of the industrial revolution, Deirdre McCloskey makes the case that liberty combined with dignity granted by society to entrepreneurs was responsible for launching the first industrial revolution.[11] The United States also had strong respect for individual liberty and property rights during its transformation. Compared with other countries in the world, the United States still does well on these margins, although not as well as it did in the nineteenth century.

Some would mistakenly conclude that the East Asian success stories of Hong Kong, Singapore, Taiwan, and South Korea are counterexamples because some of them, particularly Taiwan and South Korea, engaged in industrial planning. Although some industrial planning did occur, these countries were overwhelmingly market oriented.[12] The first year economic freedom rankings are available is 1970. In 1970, Hong Kong was ranked the most economically free country in the world, Singapore was the seventh, Taiwan sixteenth, and South Korea thirty-first (in the top 20 percent). Since that time, Hong Kong and Singapore have come to dominate the top two spots on the economic freedom index.

In recent years, China and India have also made large improvements in economic freedom. China's economic freedom score has improved by more than 50 percent since 1980, but this understates

---

[11] Deirdre McCloskey, *Bourgeois Dignity: Why Economics Can't Explain the Modern World* (Chicago: University of Chicago Press, 2010).

[12] The industrial planning that did occur actually impeded development. See Benjamin Powell, "State Development Planning: Did It Create an East Asian Miracle?" *Review of Austrian Economics* 18, No. 3/4 (2005), for an account of how planning did not promote development but economic freedom did.

China's liberalization because much of the reform has taken place on the local level and does not make it into the national data used to construct the freedom index. Similarly, since India began its reforms in 1991, its freedom score has improved by more than 25 percent. In both cases, the countries still have relatively low levels of freedom, but each illustrates how rapidly growth can be achieved with improvements in freedom.

RACE TO THE BOTTOM?

Two hundred years ago sweatshops existed in Great Britain, and they appeared soon after in the United States. As those countries grew richer, the sweatshops disappeared. Some of the textile jobs improved their wages and working conditions. Others saw their labor get bid away and moved overseas to use cheaper, more abundant labor. The same process occurred more rapidly in Hong Kong, Singapore, Taiwan, and South Korea. Now the sweatshops are located in India, China, Indonesia, Central America, and elsewhere. As these countries grow wealthier, we are likely to witness the sweatshops moving again.

Some people mistakenly view this as a race to the bottom. It is really a race to the top. Each of these countries was poor before it had sweatshops. Sweatshops came as part of the process of development. As that process played out, the countries became wealthier because the workers became more productive. With that increased productivity came increased pay and workers who were better suited to doing tasks other than low-skilled textile work. As a result, the workers were bid away from working in textiles. In some cases they were replaced with machines that made the remaining employees more productive and better paid. In other cases they were replaced in poor foreign countries with labor that had fewer valuable alternative uses.

This does not mean that some countries in the world must be doomed to sweatshop standards of living because they are the last to develop. The same process of development that occurred everywhere else can still occur in those countries. Textiles must be made somewhere. But if that location has high labor productivity, the work will be well compensated and have good working conditions. At that stage of world economic development, perhaps textile manufacturing in the former Third World will look like it does in the United States today, perhaps better. Development is not zero sum; no nation need be trapped in poverty except by its own misguided policies that prevent the process of development from happening.

CONCLUSION

Much of this book has argued that sweatshops are the best alternative available to the people who choose to work in them. That is likely a depressing fact for many readers. Simply being the best bad option for workers might not make you feel much better about buying clothes made in sweatshops. This chapter has argued that sweatshops are more than just the least bad option for workers. Sweatshops are also part of the process that will ultimately eliminate sweatshops.

Sweatshops are not new. They existed in Great Britain and the United States 150 years ago. Slowly, as our productivity increased, pay also increased and working conditions improved. Eventually the process of economic development eliminated sweatshops in Great Britain and the United States. Sweatshops are part of this development process. They require capital to be created. They often bring in new technology, and workers often build human capital on the job. Thus, sweatshops bring with them three of the proximate causes of higher productivity that eventually raises workers out of sweatshop conditions.

Unfortunately, sweatshops by themselves are not enough to guarantee a developmental path out of poverty. An institutional environment that protects private property and economic freedom is also necessary. Great Britain and the United States had that environment when they went through their transformations. So did East Asian countries that had sweatshops until recently. Some of the countries where sweatshops are located today, such as China and India, have been making large strides in improving their economic freedom, but others have not. Sweatshops will be part of their own cure in the countries that embrace economic freedom. In the countries that do not, they will remain a crutch that is the least bad option for many people.

Let us now examine what role activists might be able to play in speeding the end of sweatshops, keeping in mind the economics of sweatshop employment and role the process of development has played in ending sweatshops elsewhere.

10

What Good Can Activists Do?

At this point, some readers likely feel a bit frustrated. You might accept that the sweatshop jobs are better than the available alternatives and that they are part of the development process that will eventually lead to better jobs. But you still feel empathy for the Third World workers who toil making your apparel, and want to do something to help them. This chapter is for you. It is time to explore positive steps that activists can take to help Third World sweatshop workers.

First, before moving on to new policies, it is worth considering how your actions should change if you have been an anti-sweatshop activist in the past. Rule number one for helping Third World workers should be "Do No Harm." Using boycotts or advocating for policies that mandate higher minimum wages or better working conditions make Third World workers worse off. They unemploy the workers and change their desired mix of compensation for the worse. If you have advocated for these policies or trade sanctions against countries that do not have high standards, there is one simple constructive action you can take to help sweatshop workers: stop. With that in mind, let us take a look at some other constructive steps you might take to help poor workers in the Third World.

SPECIFICALLY TARGET SLAVE LABOR

All of the arguments in this book have focused on situations in which workers voluntarily choose to work in a sweatshop. The vast majority of sweatshops that are protested against and appear in the news fall into this category. There is, however, a minority of cases that could be considered slave labor. These situations could involve a company or government using the threat of violence to get the workers to take the job, fraud in human trafficking in which after arriving the worker's passport is confiscated so they have no ability to leave their employer without risking going to jail, or parents selling unwilling children into bondage.

Consider what Britain's *Observer* newspaper discovered at one of the Gap's subcontractors in India. A ten-year-old boy reported:

[I] was bought from my parents' village in [the northern state of] Bihar and taken to New Delhi by train. The men came looking for us in July. They had loudspeakers in the back of a car and told my parents that, if they sent me to work in the city, they won't have to work in the farms. My father was paid a fee for me, and I was brought down with 40 other children.[1]

A twelve year old reported that if any of the children cried "they would be hit with a rubber pipe or [be] punished with an oily cloth stuffed in their mouths." The children were forced to work sixteen hours a day, and they received no pay. When the Gap found out about it, the company immediately terminated its relationship with the subcontractor. In situations like this, where a child has literally been sold into slavery, it is entirely appropriate for the Gap to terminate its relationship and for activists to enact boycotts that will dry up the demand for this type of labor.

When a factory has to use the threat of violence to keep a worker, working in that factory clearly is not the worker's best alternative. Unfortunately, all too often anti-sweatshop activists, such as Jim Keady, blur the line between voluntarily chosen jobs and slavery. Keady, who specifically targets Nike, is known to appear wearing a T-shirt that reads "Slavery" with the "v" turned into a Nike Swoosh.[2] Equating voluntarily chosen low-wage manufacturing jobs with slavery does a tremendous injustice to the millions who have been held in chattel slavery throughout human history. It also confuses the debate about sweatshops today, and does an injustice to those who are still forced to toil in a state of involuntary servitude. Instead, anti-sweatshop groups should specifically target the rare instances in which slave labor is being used to produce

[1] CNN, "Gap: Report of Kids' Sweatshop 'Deeply Disturbing,'" *CNN World*, October 29, 2007, retrieved from http://articles.cnn.com/2007-10-29/world/gap.labor_1_clothing-retailer-gap-child-labor-gap-kids-stores?_s=PM:WORLD.

[2] See http://sweatfreeshop.com/sweatshop-videos/jim-keady-exposes-nike/ (accessed August 31, 2011) for one such video.

apparel. In these situations, boycotts, pressure for legal changes, and law enforcement are appropriate responses.

BUY "MADE IN THE THIRD WORLD"

People need to change their mentality that buying goods from Third World countries harmfully exploits those workers. Buying goods made by Third World labor increases the demand for that labor. More workers can be employed with increased demand, and as long as they are voluntarily choosing the job, they are demonstrating that it is better than their prior employment. Plus, with increased demand, wages can be pushed up. Consciously buying goods made by Third World workers is essentially an antiboycott.

There is no shortage of advocates for "Buy Made in America and Americans work" or "Buy Local" campaigns. I am sure there are many union members of the AFL-CIO and UNITE who believe in these campaigns at the same time their own unions are taking actions in the name of helping sweatshop workers. But Buy American and helping sweatshop workers are conflicting goals. To the extent that Buy American programs actually influence people's purchases, they harm Third World workers by decreasing the demand for their labor.

Therefore, one positive thing people could do is market their own "buy made in the Third World if you care about sweatshop workers" campaigns. Unfortunately, I doubt that such a campaign would become widely popular because it does not appeal to the same nationalist instincts that Buy American does. But one thing that the anti-sweatshop movement has been successful at is garnering public attention. This type of public awareness campaign would at least be in line with the economic interest of the sweatshop workers, even if it does not lead to much of a change in demand. Furthermore, activists themselves could follow the policy in their own shopping decisions. Would activists' purchases alone do much to change the demand for Third World labor? Probably not, but it is a start in the right direction.

"ETHICAL" BRANDING

I argued in a previous chapter that it is ethical to buy products from sweatshops, hence the quotations in this section's title. However, I do think there is a role for what activists might label ethical branding, in which companies make voluntary improvements in wages and working conditions as part of their marketing strategy.

Reforms at the level of voluntary company codes can be an inherent part of the market process that both critics of sweatshops and their defenders embrace. Explicit company codes might be voluntarily adopted when firms believe that they will increase consumer demand for their product. In this case, the explicit code and improved wages and conditions are part of a profit-maximizing marketing strategy. Consumers would have to place higher subjective valuations on these "ethically" produced goods for the strategy to work. Economists Kimberly Elliot and Richard Freeman's analysis discussed in Chapter 3 found a kinked demand for sweatshop products where consumers are price sensitive when good conditions are used as a marketing strategy.[3] This means there is little scope for many companies improving conditions from an uninformed baseline as a marketing strategy. Thus, I believe ethical branding can be successfully pursued for some products, but these products are the exception rather than the norm.

One important caution is in order when reforms come at the company-policy level. A company may pursue ethical branding by advertising that its factories have certain minimum wages and working conditions, downplaying the fact that these conditions are met only because their factories are located in relatively richer, higher-productivity countries. Remember the "Shop with a Conscience Consumer Guide" from Chapter 3? Twenty-nine of the factories are located in the United States and Canada; only eleven are located in Latin and South America, and a single factory is in Asia. Although consumers might feel they are "shopping with a conscience," they are mostly buying products made by wealthy First World union workers, decreasing the demand for products made in poorer countries and thus harming the employment prospects of the poorer Third World workers.

This points to a role that activists should embrace. The average consumer probably is not going to take the time to know which

---

[3] Kimberly Elliot and Richard Freeman, "White Hats or Don Quixotes? Human Rights Vigilantes in the Global Economy," in *Emerging Labor Market Institutions for the Twenty First Century*, eds. R. Freeman, J. Hersch, and L. Mishel (Chicago: University of Chicago Press, 2004).

"sweat-free" or "ethical" brands are actually doing something to help
Third World workers and which are merely a sham, or even worse, a
fraud such as the shop with a conscience guide that transfers wealth to
First World workers at the expense of the poor. Anti-sweatshop activists should direct energy to exposing frauds such as the shop with a
conscience guide. The National Labor Committee, which is famous for
its exposés on sweatshop conditions, should redirect its efforts to
exposing false sweat-free branding like this.

At this point, it is also worth remembering that the case for sweatshops does not depend on the claim that the market is necessarily in a
perfectly efficient general equilibrium in which all gains from exchange
have been exhausted and all information is known. The market is a
dynamic discovery procedure that always tends toward a final state of
rest (general equilibrium), but that end point is always moving as new
information is discovered, technology changes, and consumer preferences evolve. Therefore, not every voluntary action that employers
could take to improve wages and working conditions without unemploying workers has already been taken.[4]

Arnold and Hartman document what they call the "moral imagination" exercised by Adidas-Salomon and Nike management in improving
working conditions in their firms and supply chains.[5] For them, moral
imagination involves an exploratory function that lets people question
the conventional ways of doing things in their own culture as well as
utilizing and transforming norms from other cultures. The exercise of
moral imagination helps discover some of the improvements in working
conditions that the market has not yet adopted.

However, we should take care not to over-generalize from anecdotes
such as this. The mere fact that ways to improve upon current market
conditions always exist does not justify mandating standards at the

---

[4] Both Powell and Zwolinski have commended Arnold and Hartman for their work in
documenting some voluntary actions firms have taken. See Benjamin Powell, "In
Reply to Sweatshop Sophistries," *Human Rights Quarterly* 28, No. 4 (November
2006), 1031–1042; and Matt Zwolinski, "Sweatshops, Choice, and Exploitation,"
Business Ethics Quarterly 17, No. 4 (October 2007), 689–727. We also believe that
making these actions more widely known to other companies can help speed the
discovery of improvements that can take place without harming workers.

[5] Denis Arnold and Laura Hartman, "Moral Imagination and the Future of Sweatshops,"
Business and Society Review 108, No. 4 (December 2003), 425–461.

industry level. Some individual companies may find enhanced consumer demand in response to improved working conditions, whereas others do not. Some companies may find efficiency wages improve productivity, whereas others do not. A filtering process that allows reforms to take place where they help workers but does not mandate them where they do not is necessary to determine what can work and what would unemploy workers. The market's competitive process is precisely that filter.

The "moral imagination" is precisely the entrepreneurial imagination that generates profits. Although inefficiency exists in the status quo because profit-maximizing firms have not discovered all information, it is the very undiscovered nature of this knowledge that makes it crucial that reform comes from the bottom up as the knowledge is discovered. The knowledge of the particulars of time and place where particular mechanisms could improve worker welfare without unemploying others are not known to any one mind and thus cannot be imposed by regulation without also doing so in other situations in which workers would be hurt.

This is precisely where ethical branding can play a decentralized discovery role. As some firms experiment and succeed or fail, the market discovers the information that was previously unknown. Sometimes it is claimed that "defenders of sweatshops tend to ground their arguments in textbook economics, rather than in actual studies of labor markets. Few studies have been conducted of labor markets in which corporations have voluntarily increased wages."[6] Studying some markets in which firms did have the mechanisms available and raised wages does nothing to undermine the standard textbook economics that allows for their presence in some but not all situations. The assertion that "the claims of sweatshop defenders are undermined by the many corporations, in a variety of industries, that routinely expend substantial corporate resources to help ensure safe and healthy working conditions for workers" is simply false.[7] It is precisely the nonuniversal nature of the specific instances and mechanisms that makes the textbook economic defense of sweatshops correct.

---

[6] Denis Arnold, "Working Conditions: Safety and Sweatshops," in *The Oxford Handbook of Business Ethics*, eds. George Brenkert and Tom Beauchamp (New York: Oxford University Press, 2010), 645–646.

[7] Arnold, "Working Conditions," 642.

Where does this leave a role for activists in the ethical branding process? Firms will have a profit incentive to find out when ethical branding will increase profits. But this does not mean activists cannot help. Activists could undertake market research and survey consumers to try to identify where there is a market niche to be served. They could also play a role as certifiers. Many companies or organizations may claim to be practicing ethical branding, but an activist-run nonprofit (or for-profit) could serve as a sort of Good Housekeeping Seal of Approval that certifies the organization is living up to its claims of helping workers. Finally, as mentioned when discussing the shop with a conscience guide, decentralized activists could target fraudulent claims of ethical branding that do not actually help Third World workers for their protests and demonstrations.

Ultimately, however, even where ethical branding can be successful, this is probably a niche market, and one in which there will be a lot of room for fraudulent claims because a lot of consumers want to feel good about themselves, but few will actually be willing to do the work to find out if they are actually doing good. As David Vogel put it in another context,

CSR [Corporate Social Responsibility] is best understood as a niche rather than as a generic strategy: it makes business sense for some firms in some areas under some circumstances. Many of the proponents of corporate social responsibility mistakenly assume that because some companies are behaving more responsibly in some areas, some firms can be expected to behave more responsibly in more areas.[8]

TARGETED PROGRAMS FOR CHILDREN

Almost all anti-sweatshop groups are opposed to child labor, and some focus exclusively on it. Anti–child-labor resolutions are among the core labor standards of the ILO. The main cure for child labor is the process of development that raises family incomes so that children do not have to work. But activists who do not want to wait around for the process of development can take actions to help children now.

---

[8] David Vogel, *The Market for Virtue: The Potential and Limits of Corporate Social Responsibility* (Washington, DC: The Brookings Institute, 2005).

We do not make sweatshop workers, whether an adult or child, better off by taking their option of sweatshop work away. We make them better off when we give them better alternatives than sweatshop work. The best way to help children attend school rather than work in sweatshops is to pay them, either with money, food, or some other necessity, to go to school rather than work.

The Progresa program in Mexico is one such program that other countries are increasingly emulating. Under Progresa, transfers to poor households have additional cash incentives for children to go to school. The size of the cash incentive increases as children get older, to offset their greater earnings potential. Economist Paul Schultz found that rates of participation in work significantly declined with eligibility for Progresa.[9] He projects that educational attainment will rise from 6.8 years to 7.45 years because of the program. However, as Martin Ravllion and Quentin Wondon found elsewhere, sometimes educational subsidies do more to increase education than they do to decrease child labor because the two are not necessarily mutually exclusive.[10]

Some caution with these types of programs is in order. Most importantly, when instituted by governments in the countries where the sweatshops are located, these programs must ultimately be financed by taxation. As taxation stifles capital formation and job growth elsewhere, such programs would slow the process of economic development that is the ultimate cure for child labor. Furthermore, the redistribution system itself would eat up resources and be at risk of corruption.

However, the basic idea of paying children to go to school rather than work can be an effective one. If First World activists want to do something to decrease child labor, they should work for nonprofits, or form their own, that raise charitable donations for the cause. Their own NGO, with funds raised voluntarily in the First World, could then implement programs in poor countries with sweatshops that pay children to give up their sweatshop jobs and attend school instead. Raising money from concerned citizens in the First World and then offering it

[9] Paul Schultz, "School Subsidies for the Poor: Evaluating the Mexican Progresa Poverty Program," *Journal of Development Economics* 74, No. 1 (2004), 199–250.

[10] Martin Ravallion and Quentin Wodon, "Does Child Labor Displace Schooling? Evidence on Behavioral Responses to an Enrollment Subsidy," *Economic Journal* 110 (2000), C158–C175.

on a voluntary basis to children in the Third World in return for their promise not to work increases the children's options. Should they choose school funds rather than factory work, they demonstrate that the new choice is better than their previous alternative. This, unlike bans on child labor, makes them better off.

PROMOTE THE PROCESS OF DEVELOPMENT

The process of economic development has been the greatest cure for poverty in human history. If activists want to help workers, they should take actions to speed up the process of development in the countries where sweatshops locate. Unfortunately, the development process is complex and difficult to promote from the outside. But that does not mean that nothing can be done.

Economic development aid is the most common way people think they can help poor countries develop. Unfortunately, it does not work. After more than sixty years of World Bank, Organization for Economic Cooperation and Development (OECD), International Monetary Fund (IMF), and national government programs such as USAID, it is hard to assess them as anything other than a massive failure. Official government aid often goes through Third World countries' national governments. Political graft and outright theft are well-documented problems. In fact, *USA Today* published its list of the twenty worst dictators in the world. All of them received development aid from the United States or OECD.[11] But the problems with development aid are more fundamental than bad dictators stuffing their Swiss bank accounts.

As an economist and former World Bank employee, William Easterly has documented that the incentives for donors, recipient governments, and private citizens are often perverse and lead well-meaning programs to fail.[12] Another fundamental problem is that aid for investment does not work like private investment because it takes place outside of the market process and is not subject to the profit and loss test. Thus, even when aid does create capital, it is not the right capital.

---

[11] See Benjamin Powell and Matt Ryan, "Stop Aiding Dictators," *Providence Journal*, February 27, 2006, retrieved from http://www.independent.org/newsroom/article.asp?id=1682.

[12] See William Easterly, *The Elusive Quest for Growth* (Cambridge, MA: MIT Press, 2002).

Development aid has been a trivial fraction of the economy of almost all of the major development successes since World War II. At the same time, the countries that have received large aid flows have failed to develop. As economist Christopher Coyne said about Bono, there is a difference between singing about poor people and actually helping them. Development aid is a soothing song for First World citizens, but it does not actually promote development.

We saw in Chapter 8 that an institutional environment that supports private property and protects economic freedom is necessary for the process of development. Although economists have ample evidence that this environment promotes growth, they know a lot less about how to create this environment where it does not already exist. Although foreign aid programs have tried tying policy reform to the aid at times, they have not been successful in promoting an environment of economic freedom. In fact, foreign aid generally undermines economic freedom. Economist P. T. Bauer spent much of his career arguing that foreign aid "politicizes economic life" and undermines the institutions necessary for development.[13] When large aid transfers can be had from the government, entrepreneurs spend time competing to obtain the aid projects rather than innovating and competing to please consumers. Aid essentially misdirects entrepreneurship from productive activities to unproductive ones. Aid also helps create a culture in which people believe the economy centers around the state rather than the private marketplace, and as a result may lead to pressure for a state-directed economy rather than an environment of economic freedom. Economist Matt Ryan and I studied how development aid impacts economic freedom in all the countries with data available from 1970 to 2000.[14] We found that after controlling for other factors, such as a country's level of income, the larger aid was as a fraction of a country's economy over a five- or ten-year period, the lower their economic freedom level was at the end of the period.

What about military intervention? Can the U.S. armed forces displace bad governments and then install the right environment for growth

---

[13] See P. T. Bauer, *Dissent on Development* (Cambridge, MA: Harvard University Press, 1971), and *The Development Frontier* (Cambridge, MA: Harvard University Press, 1991) for two examples.

[14] Benjamin Powell and Matt Ryan, "Does Development Aid Lead to Economic Freedom?" *Journal of Private Enterprise* 22, No. 1 (Fall 2006), 1–21.

during reconstruction efforts? Economist Christopher Coyne studied all U.S. interventions and reconstruction efforts in foreign countries since 1900 to see how successful they were at installing lasting liberal democratic regimes.[15] He used the Polity IV database to measure how liberal and democratic regimes were after U.S. military interventions. He did not set the bar for success high, considering any polity as good as present-day Iran a success. Of the twenty-five reconstruction efforts for which more than five years had passed since the end of occupation, only seven scored as well as present-day Iran – a 28 percent success rate. Ten years after occupation, the rate of success remained the same, and it rose to only 39 percent fifteen years after occupation and 36 percent after twenty years. Success stories such as Japan and Germany after World War II are the exception rather than the norm.

The problem is that a new constitution establishing the right institutions is still just a piece of paper. A constitution does not enforce itself. If the existing power structure does not enforce the rules, it does not matter how good they are on paper. Economists Claudia Williamson and Carrie Kerekes found that the main constraint on state predation is the informal culture rather than the formal rules on paper.[16] Furthermore, for development, the formal institutional rules must be consistent with the ideology and culture of the local population. In other research, Williamson found that the ability of formal institutions to generate beneficial results depends on their mapping onto the informal culture.[17] This does not mean that accepting whatever the indigenous culture might be will lead to growth. There are plenty of ways to live, but not plenty that result in development. Only a culture that respects property and freedom develops. This means the game for development is changing the hearts and minds of people so that informal culture supports markets and private enterprise and forces their governments to respect the formal institutions that support this environment, as well.

---

[15] Christopher Coyne, *After War: The Political Economy of Exporting Democracy* (Palo Alto, CA: Stanford University Press, 2008).

[16] Claudia Williamson and Carrie Kerekes, "Securing Private Property: Formal versus Informal Institutions," *Journal of Law and Economics*, 54, No. 3 (2011), 537–572.

[17] Claudia Williamson, "Informal Institutions Rule: Institutional Arrangements and Economic Performance," *Public Choice* 139, No. 3 (2009), 371–387.

We must be much more humble about our ability to help a country develop from the outside once we realize that it is citizen's hearts and minds that we must ultimately capture to succeed. But this does not mean that activists cannot do anything. Circulating ideas supportive of private property and economic freedom in Third World countries is a necessary, although not sufficient, condition for getting the culture and ideology right for economic development.

The Atlas Economic Research Foundation is the world leader in spreading the ideas of free markets and individual liberty to intellectual entrepreneurs throughout the world. Sir Anthony Fischer founded Atlas in 1981. Fisher had founded the Institute of Economic Affairs, a very influential British think tank, in 1955. After he helped start-up a couple of other think tanks abroad, he created Atlas to replicate the process around the world. Atlas's mission is to "discover, develop, and support intellectual entrepreneurs worldwide who share a vision of a peaceful and prosperous society of free and responsible individuals that requires respect for the foundations of a free society: individual liberty, property rights, limited government under the rule of law, and the market order." Atlas now works with more than 400 free-market organizations in more than 80 countries. Activists concerned with the plight of workers in countries with sweatshops should consider how they could help Atlas help locals spread the ideas of liberty that are necessary for development.

Think tanks play an important role in disseminating the ideas necessary for development to the general population. But it is also important to educate the future leaders who can help spread those ideas. All too often, schooling in poor countries places little to no emphasis on understanding how market economies operate and what institutions are necessary for them to promote development. Activists could work on educational outreach programs for children. Missionary work could focus on educating in classical liberal ideas.

The most inspiring university I know of is the Universidad Francisco Marroquín. Founded in Guatemala by Manual Ayau in 1971, the university is explicitly committed to educating in the classical liberal ideas that are essential for supporting the environment necessary for economic development. The university has nearly 3,000 undergraduate students and another 1,500 graduate students. The university seeks to educate the intellectual elite of Guatemala in the hope of shaping the ideas of those who will lead the country in the future. Note that the intellectual elite does not necessarily mean the financial elite. The university actively recruits students from poor families, some of whose parents might even work in sweatshops, and provides promising students with scholarships to attend. Although economics and law have been the traditional focus of the university, it has schools of medicine, architecture, and psychology, among others. Regardless of major, all students must take one course on the thought of famed classical liberal economists Ludwig Von Mises and Friedrich Hayek. If the world had more universities such as this one, chances would be better of changing the hearts and minds of people trapped in the poorer countries around the world.

Forming think tanks and educating students does not guarantee that a country's ideology will change in favor of economic freedom, but it is a start. Ultimately, these countries have poor institutions of governance that need to change. When a break occurs in the political equilibrium that is enforcing these bad institutions, it is crucial that the right ideas are on hand and ready to be adopted.

This points to the role that crisis can play in institutional change. The usual development mantra is that aid is necessary to avert crisis. But averting crises in places with poor institutions helps those poor institutions remain in place. Sometimes a crisis provides a break in the political equilibrium that allows for the adoption of good institutions. In recent years, India, Ireland, and New Zealand, to name a few, all embarked on major liberalizations that increased economic freedom as a way to deal with their financial crises.[18] This is not to say that crisis is necessarily good. There has been no shortage of crises that result in no change or worse change. But they do provide a break and, if the right ideas are on hand, an opportunity for real reform.[19]

---

[18] For case studies of the reforms in these three countries, see Benjamin Powell, *Making Poor Nations Rich: Entrepreneurship and the Process of Development* (Palo Alto, CA: Stanford University Press, 2008).

[19] For a recent book exploring the process of political change, see Wayne Leighton and Edward Lopez, *Madmen, Intellectuals, and Academic Scribblers* (Palo Alto, CA: Stanford University Press, 2012). They argue that change occurs when academics have come up with new ideas, intellectuals have popularized them, and then external circumstances change that makes adopting those ideas in the interests of those ruling society.

Agitating for free trade is one final thing activists could do to promote the development of the Third World. Lowering trade barriers to Third World countries increases the wages that the workers who produce the imported goods can be paid. Eliminating tariffs increases the net revenue a firm receives for each good sold, which enables the same physical productivity from a worker to generate more revenue for the firm. As a result, the worker's upper bound of compensation is increased. A lowered trade barrier results in this one-time increase in income, which is reason enough for activists to support free trade. But it gets better.

It turns out that freedom is contagious. Economists have long contended that free trade promotes economic freedom. In the nineteenth century, Richard Cobden and Frederic Bastiat contended that free trade spreads economic freedom abroad by disseminating new ideas. The new ideas might be embodied in the goods themselves or they might come from how trade affects views toward market exchange compared with isolationist subsistence. It turns out they were right. When a more economically free country trades with a less economically free country, the less economically free country becomes more free. Economists Russ Sobel and Peter Leeson found that countries "catch" approximately 20 percent of their trading partners' levels and changes in economic freedom.[20] Although the impact of any one nation's freedom spreading to a trading partner may be modest, the combined effect of a larger free trade agreement that includes many trading partners of a less-free country may help create larger increases in economic freedom. Thus, activists concerned both with the immediate welfare gains for workers in sweatshop countries and ways to achieve the enabling environment for economic growth in those countries should agitate for freer trade between those countries, the United States, and other freer nations.

Economic development is the best way to improve the lives of sweatshop workers. But once we realize that development depends on getting both the correct formal institutional environment and the informal culture and ideology to support it, we must be fairly modest about how much activists, or anyone else from the outside, can do to improve

---

[20] Russell Sobel and Peter Leeson, "The Spread of Global Economic Freedom," in *Economic Freedom of the World 2007 Annual Report*, eds. James Gwartney and Robert Lawson (Vancouver, BC, Canada: The Fraser Institute, 2007).

development. The best we can hope for is the spread of ideas supportive of individual liberty, private property, and economic freedom. We can create think tanks, universities, and other educational programs to spread these ideas. We can agitate for freer trade between the United States and countries that use sweatshops in the hope that some of our free institutions will rub off on them. But ultimately, the local indigenous culture must agitate for the right changes and enforce the right institutions itself. Outsiders in the West will play only a limited role in that.

RELAX IMMIGRATION RESTRICTIONS

Third World countries are poor because they have poor institutions that do not support an environment of economic freedom. It might be hard to give them that environment from the outside, but an alternative is obvious. Let them move from their country with poor institutions to places such as the United States that have better institutions. People who immigrate to the United States from poor countries instantly experience a boost in their productivity and their standard of living. Nothing physical changes about the worker's human capital, but by matching their skills with U.S. capital, technology, complementary labor, and the enabling environment of economic freedom workers can instantly produce and earn more.

The gains in income that can accrue to a poor Third World worker from emigration dwarf anything that could be hoped to achieve by any of the policies advocated by anti-sweatshop groups, even if the laws of economics did not undermine their favored policies. Take sweatshop-hosting Haiti, for example. Economists Michael Clemens, Claudio Montenegro, and Lant Pritchett documented the wage gap between observably identical Haitians (thirty-five-year-old urban males with nine to twelve years of education born in Haiti) in the United States and Haiti.[21] They found Haitians living in the United States earned more than 1,000 percent more than similar Haitians living in Haiti. This type of gain dwarfs anything that a living wage law could achieve even if it did not unemploy workers.

---

[21] Michael Clemens, Claudio Montenegro, and Lant Pritchett, "The Place Premium: Wage Differences for Identical Workers across the U.S. Border," *Center for Global Development Working Paper* No. 148 (2008).

Some might object that when Haitians move to the United States that "Haiti" has not developed. That is true, of course. But so what? No one walks around wringing their hands worrying that Antarctica has not produced enough GDP because no humans permanently live there. We should care about human flourishing, not the amount of economic activity that takes place on a given hunk of land. To continue with the Haitian example, among those living in either the United States or Haiti, 80 percent of those who live on more than $10.00 per day live in the United States.[22] Allowing more Haitians to move to the United States may do little to raise the incomes of those who remain behind, but there is little evidence that their emigration significantly harms those left behind, either.[23] Therefore, emigration would bring a substantial increase in living standards for many without harming the nonmigrants.

The estimates of the overall gains to the world economy from more emigration are staggering. The estimates vary depending on assumptions but often range between 50 and 150 percent of world GDP if developed countries completely eliminated their barriers to immigrants.[24] Obviously, that would entail a huge movement of people, but estimates for smaller movements are also impressive. A worldwide emigration of 5 percent of the population of poor countries would boost world income by more than the gains that could be achieved from eliminating all remaining policy barriers to merchandise trade and capital flows.[25]

The main obstacle to greater emigration is the beliefs of the populations in the receiving countries. Negative opinions of immigrants often stem from misconceptions about economics. People believe that immigrants drag down the economy, steal "our" jobs, and depress our wages. Watching Lou Dobbs's economically uniformed rants about the "war on the middle class" stokes these fears.[26] But all three of these fears are misguided.

---

[22] Michael Clemens, "Economics and Emigration: Trillion-Dollar Bills on the Sidewalk?" *Journal of Economic Perspectives* 25, No. 3 (2011), 83–106.

[23] Ibid.

[24] Ibid.

[25] Ibid.

[26] I went on his show once to explain the economics of immigration. Rather than counter my arguments, he just called me names. I took it as a compliment. You can see a video of it here: http://www.youtube.com/watch?v=zoDb3D7B2Zo.

Even economists critical of immigration, such as George Borjas, find that immigration brings a net gain to the native-born population.[27] The estimated size of the net gain varies, but all estimates are small relative to the size of the economy. Immigrants also do not, steal jobs from the native born. It is obvious when an immigrant displaces a worker, and Dobbs and others can put a TV camera on the unemployed worker so that he can say, "I lost my job to an immigrant." This is a classic case of what economist Fredric Bastiat called the problem of that which is seen and that which is not.[28] The camera on the guy who lost his job is seen, but what is not seen is that another job was created precisely because of the demands for goods and services created by the immigrant. Adding more workers to the labor force simply creates more jobs. Just think of the history of the U.S. labor force since 1950. The size of the labor force has more than doubled because of the massive entry of women, baby boomers, and immigrants into the marketplace. But there is no long-term increase in unemployment. Add more workers, and we add more jobs.

Finally, immigrants do not systematically depress the wages of the native born. When economists find the wages of native-born workers depressed because of immigration, this is generally true only for those without a high school diploma, and even then the estimates are often small and sometimes nonexistent.[29] Immigration does not necessarily depress the wages of the native born for a few reasons. Immigration increases both the supply of and the demand for labor, so which effect dominates is an empirical question. Also, it is often not simply "the" supply of labor that is increased. Immigrants often have skills different from those of the native born, so they complement the natives' skills rather than substituting for them. As Adam Smith famously noted, specialization and the division of labor are limited by the extent of

---

[27] George Borjas, "Immigration," in *The Concise Encyclopedia of Economics*, ed. D. Henderson (Indianapolis: Liberty Fund, 2008).

[28] See Fredric Bastiat, *Selected Essays on Political Economy* (1848). Retrieved from the Library of Economics and Liberty http://www.econlib.org/library/Bastiat/basEss.html.

[29] For the conflicting sides of the debate, see George Borjas, "The Labor Demand Curve is Downward Sloping: Reexamining the Impact of Immigration on the Labor Market," *Quarterly Journal of Economics* 118, No. 4 (November 2003), 1335–1374; and David Card and Andrei Shleifer, "Immigration and Inequality," *American Economic Review* 99, No. 2 (2009), 1–21.

the market. Greater immigration allows a deeper market with a finer division of labor that can lead to higher living standards.

Reviewing all of the debates about immigration from the native-born perspective is beyond the scope of this chapter.[30] Beyond economics, concerns about citizenship, culture, crime, language, and numerous other issues exist. The point here is about emigration. If the welfare of Third World people, the metric we have used consistently throughout this book, is your metric, then decreasing policy barriers preventing these people from emigrating is clearly the best action First World countries can take to help these people. As an added bonus, it will also make the world, and the receiving countries, richer. Anti-sweatshop activists should join pro–open-borders activists in pushing for lower policy barriers for immigrants. Although I support this as a general policy for all, some activists narrowly concerned only with sweatshop workers could focus on policy reform that targets increased visas for those people with skills in the garment industry in countries that use sweatshops. Just do not hold your breath waiting for union-backed anti-sweatshop groups to join you in that struggle!

CONCLUSION

Just because sweatshops are the best option currently available to workers does not mean that activists can do nothing. But it does significantly change what the anti-sweatshop movement should be doing. Most of their favored policies, boycotts, trade sanctions, minimum wages, and working condition mandates need to be dropped.

Ethical branding and opposition to slave labor are two areas in which anti-sweatshop activists currently work and can still play a role. Actual slave labor should be vigorously exposed, protested, and punished. Activists can play a role in exposing fraudulent ethical branding, providing seals of approval, and discovering market demand that companies may not be aware of. In addition, activists have been concerned with child labor. Rather than banning it, they should raise

---

[30] For a survey of this literature, see R. Friedberg and J. Hunt, "The Impact of Immigrants on Host Country Wages, Employment and Growth," *Journal of Economic Perspectives* 9, No. 2 (Spring 1995), 23–44.

funds to pay children to attend school rather than work. Expanding children's options will help, but contracting their options will not.

Much of this chapter has argued for anti-sweatshop activists to completely redirect their efforts if the welfare of Third World workers is their goal. The process of economic development leads to the widespread disappearance of sweatshops. Anti-sweatshop activists should become pro-development activists. However, we have to realize how limited the ability of outsiders is to create the right environment for development in foreign countries. Despite the difficulties, activists should help spread the ideas of the freer societies to poorer ones through think tanks and other educational efforts. They should agitate for their own governments to adopt freer trade with poorer countries in the hope that trade will provide an avenue for our institutions to be exported abroad.

Finally, anti-sweatshop activists should become pro-immigration activists. A sweatshop worker, or any poor citizen of the Third World, will increase their living standards more by moving to the United States than any policy could ever hope to achieve for them in their own country.

There is a role for activists. But with an understanding of economics, that role is turned on its head from what much of the movement has done since the 1990s. If anti-sweatshop activists become advocates for free markets in goods, labor, and capital they can do more to help Third World workers than any policy for which they have previously agitated would do.

11

Conclusion

Thus far, the anti-sweatshop movement has not been particularly successful in getting their favored policies mandated. Sociologist and activist Jill Esbenshade summarizes the progress of the movement as of 2004: "Although this movement has brought the issue of sweatshops into the consuming public's eye, it has had considerably less success in translating this heightened concern into victories for garment workers in their factories."[1] Seven years later, the situation was not much different. In 2011, political scientist Shae Garwood wrote:

The anti-sweatshop network has been successful in ... raising awareness and agenda setting. The network as has also influenced the industry's adoption of the discourse of responsibility and workers' rights.... As a result of anti-sweatshop advocacy, some targeted corporations have implemented internal social auditing programs.... However, the anti-sweatshop network has been unable to achieve ... behavioral change by manufacturers. This means that workers' rights and working conditions, as articulated in the WRC code, remain largely unfulfilled.[2]

The main message of this book is that the anti-sweatshop movement's failure to mandate policies such as minimum wages and working standards is a victory for the sweatshop workers. If the activists had their way, the workers would be worse off.

Straightforward economic reasoning explains why sweatshop jobs are jeopardized by many of the actions taken by First World anti-sweatshop

---

[1] Jill Esbenshade, *Monitoring Sweatshops: Workers, Consumers, and the Global Apparel Industry* (Philadelphia: Temple University Press, 2004), 202.
[2] Shae Garwood, *Advocacy across Borders: NGOs, Anti-Sweatshop Activism, and the Global Garment Industry* (Sterling, VA: Kumarian Press, 2011), 184.

activists. However, because workers choose to work at these firms we
know that the workers believe the jobs are the best available alternative
for them. Agitating for policies that would take the option of sweatshop
employment away from these workers makes the workers worse off. It
throws them into a worse alternative now and it undermines the process
of economic development that ultimately leads to better paying jobs
with better working conditions.

The economics surrounding sweatshop employment is simple. But
as economist Peter Boettke has often said, simple economics should
not be confused with simpleminded economics. As he put it:

> [It is] the case that economics in the hands of its finest practitioners is little
> more than applied common sense. As Frank Knight pointed out, "The serious
> fact is that the bulk of the really important things that economics has to teach
> are things that people would see for themselves if they were willing to see. And
> it is hard to believe in the utility of trying to teach what men refuse to learn or
> even seriously listen to."[3]

Joshua Brown, a sweatshop monitor in the late 1990s, illustrates Knight's
insight. He was auditing a Chinese factory. As he describes it:

> We find almost every violation in the book. The workers are pulling 90-hour
> weeks. The place has no fire extinguishers or fire exits, and is so jammed full of
> material that a small fire could explode into an inferno within a minute. There
> are no safety guards on the sewing machines, and the first-aid box holds only
> packages of instant noodles.
>
> With the bosses out of earshot, I fully expect the workers to pour out their
> sorrows to me, to beg me to tell the consumers of America to help them out of
> their misery. I'm surprised at what I hear.
>
> "I'm happy to have this job," is the essence of what several workers tell me.
> "At home, I'm a drain on my family's resources. But now, I can send them
> money every month."
>
> I point out that they make only $100 a month; they remind me this is about
> five times what they can make in their home province. I ask if they feel like
> they're being exploited, having to work 90 hours a week. They laugh.
>
> "We all work piece rate here. More work, more money."

---

[3] Peter Boettke, *Living Economics: Yesterday, Today, and Tomorrow* (Oakland: The
Independent Institute, 2012), 19–20; and Frank Knight, "The Role of Principles in
Economics and Politics," in *Selected Essays of Frank H. Knight*, Vol. 2, ed. Ross
Emmett (Chicago: University of Chicago Press, 1999), 364.

The worst part of the day for them, it seemed, was seeing me arrive. "I don't want to tell you anything because you'll close my factory and ruin any chances I have at having a better life one day," one tells me.[4]

When Joshua left the factory, he told "the owner that she needs to buy fire extinguishers, put actual first-aid supplies in the first-aid kits, install safety equipment on the sewing machines, and reduce worker hours to below 60 per week."[5] Joshua Brown refused to learn from, and seriously listen to, the sweatshop employees he interviewed.

If you have made it to this point in the book, I appreciate the fact that you have seriously listened to what economics has to say about sweatshops. Economist Henry Simons said, "Economics is primarily useful, both to the student and to the political leader, as a prophylactic against popular fallacies."[6] It is my sincere hope that this book, however marginally, will serve as such a prophylactic and will dissuade people from agitating for policies that would jeopardize sweatshop jobs and instead redirect people's efforts toward supporting the free enterprise system that ultimately drives the process of development that will improve the lives of sweatshop workers and their descendants.

---

[4] Joshua Brown, quoted in Esbenshade, *Monitoring Sweatshops*, 212–213.

[5] Joshua Brown, quoted in Esbenshade, *Monitoring Sweatshops*, 213.

[6] Henry Simons, *Simons' Syllabus*, ed. Gordon Tullock (Fairfax, VA: Center for the Study of Public Choice, 1983), 3.

References

Academic Consortium on International Trade. "Sweatshop Letter." Retrieved from http://www.fordschool.umich.edu/rsie/acit/Documents/July29Sweat shopLetter.pdf

Alta Gracia, "What is a Living Wage?" Retrieved from http://altagraciaap parel.com/story

American Center for International Labor Solidarity. http://www.solidaritycen ter.org

American Federation of Labor-Congress of Industrial Organizations. http://www.aflcio.org

Arnold, Denis. "Philosophical Foundations: Moral Reasoning, Human Rights, and Global Labor Practices." In *Rising above Sweatshops: Innovative Approaches to Global Labor Challenges*, edited by Laura Hartman, Denis Arnold, and Richard E. Wokutch. Westport, CT: Praeger, 2003: 77–101.

"Working Conditions: Safety and Sweatshops." In *The Oxford Handbook of Business Ethics*, edited by George Brenkert and Tom Beauchamp. New York: Oxford University Press, 2010: 371–399.

Arnold, Denis and Norman Bowie. "Sweatshops and Respect for Persons." *Business Ethics Quarterly* 13, No. 2 (April 2003): 221–242.

"Respect for Workers in Global Supply Chains: Advancing the Debate over Sweatshops." *Business Ethics Quarterly* 17, No. 1 (January 2007): 135–145.

Arnold, Denis and Laura Hartman. "Beyond Sweatshops: Positive Deviancy and Global Labour Practices." *Business Ethics: A European Review* 14, No. 3 (July 2005): 206–222.

"Moral Imagination and the Future of Sweatshops." *Business and Society Review* 108, No. 4 (December 2003): 425–461.

"Worker Rights and Low Wage Industrialization: How to Avoid Sweatshops." *Human Rights Quarterly* 28, No. 3 (August 2006): 676–700.

Asshagrie, Kebebew. "Statistics on Working Children and Hazardous Child Labour in Brief." Geneva: International Labor Office, 1997.

Associated Press. "Factory in Bangladesh Lost Fire Clearance before Blaze." *New York Times*, December 7, 2012. Retrieved from http://www.nytimes.com/2012/12/08/world/asia/bangladesh-factory-where-dozens-died-was-illegal.html?_r=0

Barzel, Yoram. "A Theory of Rationing by Waiting." *Journal of Law and Economics* 17 (1974): 73–95.

Bastiat, Frederic. *Selected Essays on Political Economy* (1848). Retrieved from http://www.econlib.org/library/Bastiat/basEss.html

Basu, Kaushik. "Child Labor: Cause, Consequence, and Cure, with Remarks on International Labor Standards." *Journal of Economic Literature* 37, No. 3 (September 1999): 1083–1119.

Bauer, P. T. *Dissent on Development*. Cambridge, MA: Harvard University Press, 1971.

The Development Frontier. Cambridge, MA: Harvard University Press, 1991.

Baumol, William. "Entrepreneurship: Productive, Unproductive, and Destructive." *Journal of Political Economy* 98, No. 5 (October 1990): 893–921.

Berggren, N. "The Benefits of Economic Freedom." *The Independent Review* 8, No. 2 (Fall 2003): 193–211.

Bisseker, Claire. "Clothing Industry. Policy Doesn't Fit Practice." *Financial Mail* (South Africa), September 10, 2010.

Boettke, Peter. *Living Economics: Yesterday, Today, and Tomorrow*. Oakland: The Independent Institute, 2012.

Borjas, George. "Immigration." In *The Concise Encyclopedia of Economics*, edited by David Henderson. Indianapolis: Liberty Fund, 2008: 254–256.

"The Labor Demand Curve is Downward Sloping: Reexamining the Impact of Immigration on the Labor Market." *Quarterly Journal of Economics* 118, No. 4 (November 2003): 1335–1374.

Brown, Drusilla, Alan Deardorff, and Robert Stern. "Child Labor: Theory, Evidence and Policy." In *International Labor Standards: History, Theories and Policy*, edited by K. Basu, H. Horn, L. Roman, and J. Shapiro. Oxford: Basil Blackwell, 2003.

Busse, Matthias. "On the Determinants of Core Labor Standards: The Case of Developing Countries." *Economics Letters* 83, No. 2 (May 2004): 211–217.

Card, David and Alan Krueger. *Myth and Measurement: The New Economics of the Minimum Wage*. Princeton: Princeton University Press, 1995.

Card, David and Andrei Shleifer. "Immigration and Inequality." *American Economic Review* 99, No. 2 (2009): 1–21.

Carson, Kevin. "Vulgar Libertarianism." Mutualist Blog: Free Market Anti-Capitalism, January 11, 2005. Retrieved from http://mutualist.blogspot.com/2005/01/vulgar-libertarianism-watch-part-1.html

Chang, Jack. "Bolivians Fail to Find Better Life in Brazil; Bolivians Are Migrating to Brazil in Search of a Better Life, but Many End Up Working under Harsh Conditions and Earning Low Pay." *Miami Herald*, December 28, 2007.

Chartier, Gary. "Sweatshops, Labor Rights, and Competitive Advantage." *Oregon Review of International Law* 10, No. 1 (September 2008): 149–188.

Clark, J. R. and Benjamin Powell. "Sweatshop Working Conditions and Employee Welfare: Say It Ain't Sew." *Comparative Economic Studies* 55 (2013): 343–357.

Clarke, Natalie. "The True Price of the £6 Dress." *The Daily Mail*, September 13, 2007. Retrieved from http://www.dailymail.co.uk/femail/article-481538/The-true-price-6-dress.html

Clean Clothes Campaign. http://www.cleanclothes.org

Clemens, Michael. "Economics and Emigration: Trillion-Dollar Bills on the Sidewalk?" *Journal of Economic Perspectives* 25, No. 3 (Summer 2011): 83–106.

Clemens, Michael, Claudio Montenegro, and Lant Pritchett. "The Place Premium: Wage Differences for Identical Workers across the U.S. Border." *Center for Global Development Working Paper* No. 148 (2008).

CNN. "Gap: Report of Kids' Sweatshop 'Deeply Disturbing.'" *CNN World*, October 29, 2007. Retrieved from http://articles.cnn.com/2007-10-29/world/gap.labor_1_clothing-retailer-gap-child-labor-gap-kids-stores?_s=PM:WORLD

Collier, Paul. "Haiti: From Natural Catastrophe to Economic Security." *A Report for the Secretary-General of the United Nations*, January 2009. Retrieved from http://www.focal.ca/pdf/haiticollier.pdf

Cowen, Tyler and Alex Tabbarrok. *Modern Principles: Macroeconomics*. New York: Worth Publishers, 2009.

Coyne, Christopher. *After War: The Political Economy of Exporting Democracy*. Palo Alto, CA: Stanford University Press, 2008.

Deere, Donald Riche, Kevin Murphy, and Finis Welch. "Sense and Nonsense on the Minimum Wage." *Regulation* 18, No. 1 (1995): 47–56.

Easterly, William. *The Elusive Quest for Growth*. Cambridge, MA: MIT Press, 2002.

Edmonds, Eric. "Does Child Labor Decline with Improving Economic Status?" *Journal of Human Resources* 40, No. 1 (Winter 2005): 77–99.

Edmonds, Eric and Nina Pavcnik. "Child Labor in the Global Economy." *Journal of Economic Perspectives* 19, No. 1 (Winter 2005): 199–220.

Elliot, Kimberly and Richard Freeman. "White Hats or Don Quixotes? Human Rights Vigilantes in the Global Economy." In *Emerging Labor Market Institutions for the Twenty First Century*, edited by R. Freeman, J. Hersch, and L. Mishel. Chicago: University of Chicago Press, 2004: 47–98.

Elliott, Kimberly, Gary Hufbauer, and Barbara Oegg. "Sanctions." In *The Concise Encyclopedia of Economics*, edited by David Henderson, 2008. Retrieved from http://econlib.org/library/Enc/Sanctions.html

Esbenshade, Jill. *Monitoring Sweatshops: Workers, Consumers, and the Global Apparel Industry.* Philadelphia: Temple University Press, 2004.

Fair Labor Association. http://www.fairlabor.org

Featherstone, Liza and United Students Against Sweatshops. *Students Against Sweatshops.* New York: Verso, 2002.

Fishback, Price. *Government and the American Economy: A New History.* Chicago: University of Chicago Press, 2007.

——— "Operations of 'Unfettered' Labor Markets: Exit and Voice in American Labor Markets at the Turn of the Century." *Journal of Economic Literature* 36, No. 2 (June 1998): 722–765.

Forbes Magazine. "America's Deadliest Jobs." http://www.forbes.com/2007/08/13/dangerous-jobs-fishing-lead-careerscx_tvr_0813danger.html

Friedberg, R. and J. Hunt. "The Impact of Immigrants on Host Country Wages, Employment and Growth." *Journal of Economic Perspectives* 9, No. 2 (Spring 1995): 23–44.

Friedman, Milton and Rose Friedman. *Two Lucky People.* Chicago: University of Chicago Press, 1998.

Garwood, Shae. *Advocacy across Borders: NGOs, Anti-Sweatshop Activism, and the Global Garment Industry.* Sterling, VA: Kumarian Press, 2011.

Goldin, Claudia and Larry Katz. "Mass Secondary Schooling and the State: The Role of State Compulsion and the High School Movement." *NBER Working Paper* No. 10075 (2003).

Goodin, Robert E. "Exploiting a Situation and Exploiting a Person." In *Modern Theories of Exploitation*, edited by Andrew Reeve. London: Sage, 1987: 166–200.

Green, Leslie. *Legal Obligation and Authority.* In *Stanford Encyclopedia of Philosophy*, Stanford University, October 1, 2010. Retrieved from http://plato.stanford.edu/entries/legalobligation

Gwartney, James, Robert Lawson, and Joshua Hall. *Economic Freedom of the World Annual Report.* Vancouver, BC, Canada: The Fraser Institute, 2011.

Hall, Joshua and Peter Leeson. "Good for the Goose, Bad for the Gander: International Labor Standards and Comparative Development." *Journal of Labor Research* 28, No. 4 (September 2007): 658–676.

Harrison, Ann and Jason Scorse. "Multinationals and Anti-Sweatshop Activism." *American Economic Review* 100, No. 1 (2010): 247–273.

Hayek, Friedrich. "Competition as a Discovery Procedure." *Quarterly Journal of Austrian Economics* 5, No. 3 (1968, 2002): 9–23.

——— "The Use of Knowledge in Society." *American Economic Review* 35, No. 4 (September 1945): 519–530.

Heady, Christopher. "The Effect of Child Labor on Learning Achievement." *World Development* 31, No. 3 (2003): 385–398.

Henderson, David. "The Case for Sweatshops." Hoover Institution, Stanford University, February 7, 2000. Retrieved from http://www.hoover.org/news/daily-report/24617

Hersch, Joni. "Compensating Differentials for Sexual Harassment." *American Economic Review Papers and Proceedings*, May 2011. Retrieved from http://papers.ssrn.com/sol3/papers.cfm?abstract_id=1743691

Institute for Global Labour and Human Rights. "Alert – Violation of CAFTA at Sam Bridge SA Guatemala," October 21, 2007. Retrieved from http://www.nlcnet.org/alerts?id=0072

Institute for Global Labour and Human Rights. "Major Worker Rights Victory in Guatemala," October 13, 2009. Retrieved from http://www.nlcnet.org/alerts?id=0022

Institute for Global Labour and Human Rights. "Women Exploiting Women," February 25, 2009. Retrieved from http://www.nlcnet.org/reports?id=0535

International Labor Organization. "Declaration on Fundamental Principles and Rights at Work." 1998. Retrieved from http://www.ilo.org/declaration/lang--en/index.htm

Every Child Counts: New Global Estimates on Child Labour. Geneva: ILO, 2002.

"Safety and Health at Work." Retrieved from http://www.ilo.org/global/topics/safety-and-health-at-work/lang--en/index.htm

"Summary of the Results of the Child and Adolescent Labour Survey in Costa Rica." 2004. Retrieved from http://www.ilo.org/ipec/ChildlabourstatisticsSIMPOC/Questionnairessurveysandreports/lang--en/index.htm

"Summary of the Results of the Child Labour Survey in El Salvador." 2004. Retrieved from http://www.ilo.org/ipec/ChildlabourstatisticsSIMPOC/Questionnairessurveysandreports/lang--en/index.htm

"Summary of the Results of the National Child Labour Survey in the Dominican Republic." 2004. Retrieved from http://www.ilo.org/ipec/ChildlabourstatisticsSIMPOC/Questionnairessurveysandreports/lang--en/index.htm

International Labor Rights Forum. http://www.laborrights.org

Irwin, Doug. *Free Trade Under Fire*. Princeton: Princeton University Press, 2002.

Kaufman, Leslie and David Gonzalez. "Labor Standards Clash with Global Reality." *New York Times*, April 24, 2001. Retrieved from http://www.nytimes.com/learning/teachers/featured_articles/20010425wednesday.html

Keady, Jim. "When Will Nike 'Just Do It' on the Sweatshop Issue?" *Huffington Post*, October 2, 2009.

Kleen, Michael. "Sweatshops and Social Justice: Can Compassionate Libertarians Agree?" Center for a Stateless Society, November 17, 2011. Retrieved from http://c4ss.org/content/8840

Knight, Frank. "The Role of Principles in Economics and Politics." *American Economic Review* 41 (1951): 1–29.

Kristof, Nicholas. "Inviting All Democrats." *New York Times*, January 14, 2004. Retrieved from http://www.nytimes.com/2004/01/14/opinion/inviting-all-democrats.html

"My Sweatshop Column." *New York Times*, January 14, 2009. Retrieved from http://kristof.blogs.nytimes.com/2009/01/14/my-sweatshop-column/

"Where Sweatshops Are a Dream." *New York Times*, January 14, 2009. Retrieved from http://www.nytimes.com/2009/01/15/opinion/15kristof.html?_r=0

Krueger, Alan. "International Labor Standards and Trade." In *Annual World Bank Conference on Development Economics 1996*, edited by M. Bruno and B. Pleskovic. Washington, DC: The World Bank, 1997, 281–302.

Krugman, Paul. "In Praise of Cheap Labor: Bad Jobs at Bad Wages Are Better Than No Jobs at All." *Slate Magazine*, March 1997. Retrieved from http://www.unz.org/Pub/Slate-1997mar-00049

"Reckonings; Hearts and Heads." *New York Times*, April 22, 2001. Retrieved from http://www.nytimes.com/2001/04/22/opinion/reckonings-hearts-and-heads.html

Leighton, Wayne and Edward Lopez. *Madmen, Intellectuals, and Academic Scribblers*. Palo Alto: Stanford University Press, 2012.

Leonard, Thomas. "Protecting Family and Race: The Progressive Case for Regulating Women's Work." *American Journal of Economics and Sociology* 64, No. 3 (2005): 757–791.

Levinson, Jeff, ed. *Mill Girls of Lowell*. Boston: History Compass, 2007.

Lindert, Peter and Jeffrey Williamson. "English Workers' Living Standards during the Industrial Revolution: A New Look." In *The Economics of the Industrial Revolution*, edited by Joel Mokyr. New Jersey: Rowman and Allanheld, 1985: 1–25.

Lindsay, Samuel. "Child Labor in the United States." *American Economic Association* 8 (February 1907): 256–259.

Lowell Offering, The. 1841.

Lowell Textile Workers Petition. *Voice of Industry*, January 15, 1845.

Maquila Solidarity Network. http://en.maquilasolidarity.org

Margolis, Mac. "Roads to Nowhere; More and More Migrants from Poor Countries Are Heading to Other Former Backwaters for Work." *Newsweek*, September 11, 2006. Retrieved from http://www.questia.com/library/1G1-150914427/roads-to-nowhere-more-and-more-migrants-from-poor

Mayer, Robert. "Sweatshops, Exploitation, and Moral Responsibility." *Journal of Social Philosophy* 38, No. 4 (2007): 605–619.

"What's Wrong with Exploitation?" *Journal of Applied Philosophy* 24, No. 2 (2007): 137–150.

McCloskey, Deirdre. *Bourgeois Dignity: Why Economics Can't Explain the Modern World*. Chicago: University of Chicago Press, 2010.

"The Industrial Revolution 1780–1860: A Survey." In *The Economics of the Industrial Revolution*, edited by Joel Mokyr. New Jersey: Rowman and Allanheld, 1985.

Meyers, Chris. "Wrongful Beneficence: Exploitation and Third World Sweatshops." *Journal of Social Philosophy* 35, No. 3 (2004): 319–333.

Miller, John. "Why Economists Are Wrong about Sweatshops and the Anti-Sweatshop Movement." *Challenge* 47, No. 1 (January/February 2003): 93–122.

Mises, Ludwig Von. *Economic Calculation in the Socialist Commonwealth*. Auburn, AL: Ludwig Von Mises Institute, 1920, 1990.

Human Action. Auburn, AL: Ludwig Von Mises Institute, 1949, 1998.

Moehling, Carolyn. "State Child Labor Laws and the Decline in Child Labor." *Explorations in Economic History* 36, No. 1 (1999): 72–106.

Mokyr, Joel. *The Enlightened Economy: An Economic History of Britain, 1700–1850*. New Haven: Yale University Press, 2009.

Moore, Michael and Kip Viscusi. *Compensation Mechanisms for Job Risks*. Princeton: Princeton University Press, 1990.

Munger, Michael. "Euvoluntary or Not, Exchange Is Just." *Social Philosophy and Policy* 28, No. 2 (Summer 2011): 192–211.

National Labor Committee. http://www.nlcnet.org

"Major Worker Rights Victory in Guatemala." October 2009. Retrieved from http://www.nlcnet.org/alerts?id=0022

"Violation of CAFTA at Sam Bridge SA Guatemala." October 2007. Retrieved from http://www.nlcnet.org/alerts?id=0072

National Labor Committee. "Child Labor: 11 year-old Halima Sews Clothing for Hanes." Retrieved from http://www.youtube.com/watch?v=pTIfY9SmJdA

National Park Service. *Lowell: The Story of an Industrial City. Official National Park Handbook, Handbook 140*. Division of Publications National Park Service. Washington, DC: U.S. Department of the Interior, 1992.

Neumark, David and William Wascher. *Minimum Wages*. Cambridge, MA: MIT Press, 2008.

O'Connor, Anne-Marie. "The Plight of Women Around the World; Central America; Labor: Sweatshops Meet U.S. Consumer Demand." *The Atlanta Journal Constitution*, September 3, 1995.

Pearce, Fred. *The Land Grabbers: The New Fight Over Who Owns the Earth*. Boston: Beacon Press, 2012.

Pierson, David. "An Influx of Illegal Workers; Sound Familiar? It's Happening in China, Where the Pay Looks Good to Vietnamese." *Los Angeles Times*, September 19, 2010.

Pollin, Robert, Justine Burns, and James Heintz. "Global Apparel Production and Sweatshop Labor: Can Raising Retail Prices Finance Living Wages?" *Cambridge Journal of Economics* 28, No. 2 (2004): 153–171.

Powell, Benjamin. "East Asian State Development Planning: Did It Create an East Asian Miracle." *Review of Austrian Economics* 18, No. 3/4 (2005): 305–323.

"In Reply to Sweatshop Sophistries." *Human Rights Quarterly* 28, No. 4 (November 2006): 1031–1042.

ed. *Making Poor Nations Rich: Entrepreneurship and the Process of Development*. Palo Alto, CA: Stanford University Press, 2008.

"Some Implications of Capital Heterogeneity." In *Handbook on Contemporary Austrian Economics*, edited by Peter Boettke. Cheltenham, UK: Edward Elgar, 2010: 124–135.

Powell, Benjamin and David Skarbek. "Sweatshop Wages and Third World Workers: Are the Jobs Worth the Sweat?" *Journal of Labor Research* 27, No. 2 (Spring 2006): 263–274.

Powell, Benjamin and Matt Ryan. "Does Development Aid Lead to Economic Freedom?" *Journal of Private Enterprise* 22, No. 1 (Fall 2006): 1–21.

"Stop Aiding Dictators." *Providence Journal*, February 27, 2006. Retrieved from http://www.independent.org/newsroom/article.asp?id=1682

Powell, Benjamin and Matt Zwolinski. "The Ethical and Economic Case against Sweatshop Labor: A Critical Assessment." *Journal of Business Ethics* 107, No. 4 (2012): 449–472.

Ravallion, Martin and Quentin Wodon. "Does Child Labor Displace Schooling? Evidence on Behavioral Responses to an Enrollment Subsidy." *Economic Journal* 110 (2000): C158–C175.

Rawls, John. *A Theory of Justice*. Cambridge, MA: Harvard University Press, 1971.

Reed, Lawrence. "Child Labor and the British Industrial Revolution." *The Freeman* 41, No. 8 (August 1991). http://www.fee.org/the_freeman/detail/child-labor-and-the-british-industrial-revolution/#axzz2bCgbEqL4

Riper, Tom Van. "America's Most Dangerous Jobs," *Forbes*, August 13, 2007. Retrieved from http://www.forbes.com/2007/08/13/dangerous-jobs-fishing-lead-careers-cx_tvr_0813danger.html

Rottenberg, Simon, ed. *The Economics of Legal Minimum Wages*. Washington, DC: American Enterprise Institute, 1981.

Sachs, Jeffrey. *The End of Poverty: Economic Possibilities for Our Time*. New York: Penguin Press, 2005.

Sample, Ruth. *Exploitation: What It Is and Why It's Wrong*. New York: Rowman and Littlefield, 2003.

Samuelson, Paul. *Economics*, 9th ed. New York: McGraw-Hill, 1973.

Scholars Against Sweatshop Labor. *Statement*. October 2001. Retrieved from http://www.peri.umass.edu/253/

Schultz, Paul. "School Subsidies for the Poor: Evaluating the Mexican Progresa Poverty Program." *Journal of Development Economics* 74, No. 1 (2004): 199–250.

Simons, Henry. *Simons' Syllabus*, edited by Gordon Tullock. Fairfax, VA: Center for the Study of Public Choice, 1983.

Skarbek, David, Emily Skarbek, Brian Skarbek, and Erin Skarbek. "Sweatshops, Opportunity Costs, and Non-Monetary Compensation: Evidence from El Salvador." *American Journal of Economics and Sociology* 71, No. 3 (2012): 539–561.

Snyder, Jeremy C. "Efficiency, Equality, and Price Gouging: A Response to Zwolinski." *Business Ethics Quarterly* 19, No. 2 (April 2009): 303–306.

"Exploitation and Sweatshop Labor: Perspectives and Issues." *Business Ethics Quarterly* 20, No. 2 (April 2010): 187–213.

"Needs Exploitation." *Ethical Theory and Moral Practice* 11, No. 4 (2008): 389–405.

Sobel, Russell and Peter Leeson. "The Spread of Global Economic Freedom." In *Economic Freedom of the World 2007 Annual Report*, edited by James Gwartney and Robert Lawson. Vancouver, BC, Canada: The Fraser Institute, 2007: 29–37.

Sollars, G. and F. Englander. "Sweatshops: Kant and Consequences." *Business Ethics Quarterly* 17, No. 1 (January 2007): 115–133.

Stearns, Peter. *The Industrial Revolution in World History*, 3rd ed. Boulder: Westview Press, 2007.

Stern, R. and K. Terrel. "Labor Standards and the World Trade Organization." *University of Michigan, Ann Arbor, RSIE Discussion Paper* No. 499 (2003).

STITCH. http://www.stitchonline.org

Stringham, Edward. "Economic Value and Costs Are Subjective." In *Handbook on Contemporary Austrian Economics*, edited by Peter Boettke. Cheltenham, UK: Edward Elgar, 2010: 43–66.

Students Against Sweatshops. http://www.studentsagainstsweatshops.org.uk

Sweat Free Communities Campaign. http://www.sweatfree.org

UNICEF. "The State of the World's Children." 1997. Retrieved from http://www.unicef.org/sowc97/

United Students Against Sweatshops. http://usas.org/

U.S. Department of Labor. Bureau of International Labor Affairs, 1994 Child Labor Report, Bangladesh. Retrieved from http://www.dol.gov/ilab/media/reports/iclp/sweat/bangladesh.htm/

U.S. Labor Education in the Americas Project. http://www.usleap.org

Valdman, Mikhail. "Exploitation and Injustice." *Social Theory and Practice: An International and Interdisciplinary Journal of Social Philosophy* 34, No. 4 (October 2008): 551–572.

"A Theory of Wrongful Exploitation." *Philosophers' Imprint* 9, No. 6 (July 2009): 1–14.

Viederman, Dan. "Any Job Is a Good Job? Think Again." *Huffington Post*, February 18, 2011.

Viscusi, Kip, Joseph Harrington, and John Vernon. *Economics of Regulation and Antitrust*, 4th ed. Cambridge, MA: MIT Press, 2005.

Vogel, David. *The Market for Virtue: The Potential and Limits of Corporate Social Responsibility*. Washington, DC: The Brookings Institute, 2005.

War on Want. http://www.waronwant.org

Wertheimer, Alan. *Exploitation*. Princeton: Princeton University Press, 1996.

"Matt Zwolinski's 'Choosing Sweatshops': A Commentary." Unpublished Manuscript. Presented at the Arizona Current Research Workshop, January 2007.

"Matt Zwolinski's 'Choosing Sweatshops': A commentary." Unpublished manuscript. Presented at the Arizona Current Research Workshop in Tuscon, AZ, January 2005.

Whaples, R. *Child Labor in the United States*. In EH.Net Encyclopedia. 2005. Retrieved from http://eh.net/encyclopedia/article/whaples.childlabor

Whitehead, Jennifer. "Topshop Faces Accusations of Using Sweatshop Labour." *Brand Republic*, August 14, 2007. Retrieved from http://www.prweek.com/uk/news/731169/Topshop-faces-accusations-using-sweatshop-labour/?DCMP=ILC-SEARCH

Williamson, Claudia. "Informal Institutions Rule: Institutional Arrangements and Economic Performance." *Public Choice* 139, No. 3 (2009): 371–387.

Williamson, Claudia and Carrie Kerekes. "Securing Private Property: Formal versus Informal Institutions." *Journal of Law and Economics* 54, No. 3 (2011): 537–572.

Wolff, Robert Paul. *In Defense of Anarchism*, 3rd ed. Berkeley: University of California Press, 1970.

Wood, Allen W. "Exploitation." *Social Philosophy and Policy* 12, No. 2 (1995): 136–158.

The Worker Rights Consortium. http://www.workersrights.org

World Bank. *World Development Indicators Online*. http://data.worldbank.org/

Yakovlev, Pavel and Russell S. Sobel. "Occupational Safety and Profit Maximization: Friends or Foes?" *Journal of Socio-Economics* 39, No. 3 (June 2010): 429–435.

Young, Iris Marion. "Responsibility and Global Justice: A Social Connection Model." *Social Philosophy and Policy* 23, No. 1 (January 2006): 102–130.

Zwolinski, Matt. "The Ethics of Price Gouging." *Business Ethics Quarterly* 18, No. 3 (July 2008): 347–378.

"Price Gouging, Non-Worseness, and Distributive Justice." *Business Ethics Quarterly* 19, No. 2 (April 2009): 295–306.

"Structural Exploitation." *Social Philosophy and Policy* 29, No. 1 (Winter 2012): 154–179.

"Sweatshops, Choice, and Exploitation." *Business Ethics Quarterly* 17, No. 4 (October 2007): 689–727.

"Exploitation and Neglect." San Diego: University of San Diego, Department of Philosophy, 2012.

About the Author

Benjamin Powell, PhD, is the director of the Free Market Institute at Texas Tech University and a visiting professor in the Rawls College of Business at TTU. He is also a Senior Fellow with the Independent Institute and a past president of the Association of Private Enterprise Education. He has written more than fifty scholarly articles and policy studies and edited two books, including *Making Poor Nations Rich: Entrepreneurship and the Process of Development*. His research on sweatshops has been reported in the *New York Times* and the *Wall Street Journal*, among other outlets.

Professor Powell regularly communicates economic concepts to popular audiences. His writing has appeared in numerous outlets, including *Investor's Business Daily*, the *Financial Times* (London), the *Christian Science Monitor*, the *Washington Post*, and the *Boston Herald*. He has appeared on *CNN, ABC, BBC, MSNBC, Showtime, CNBC, C-Span*, and was a frequent guest on *Fox Business*'s "Freedom Watch." He lectures and debates regularly at universities throughout the country. He currently writes a monthly column at the *Huffington Post*.

Professor Powell earned his BS in finance and economics at University of Massachusetts–Lowell and his MA and PhD in economics at George Mason University. Prior to joining Texas Tech he taught at Suffolk University and San Jose State University.

Index

175